POEMS *of the Old West*

POEMS
of the Old West

A ROCKY MOUNTAIN ANTHOLOGY

SELECTED AND EDITED BY

LEVETTE J. DAVIDSON

Granger Index Reprint Series

BOOKS FOR LIBRARIES PRESS
FREEPORT, NEW YORK

LIBRARY OF CONGRESS CATALOG CARD NUMBER:

68-58824

MANUFACTURED
BY
HALLMARK LITHOGRAPHERS, INC.
IN THE U.S.A.

ACKNOWLEDGMENTS

The editor is especially indebted to the following for valuable assistance in securing books, editing selections, and preparing notes about authors: Miss Ina T. Aulls, of the Western Regional History Department of the Denver Public Library; Mr. Frank Merchant, graduate assistant in the Department of English, University of Denver, 1949-51; Mrs. Agnes Wright Spring, Acting Historian, State Historical Society of Colorado; and Miss Frances Shay, Librarian of the State Historical Society of Colorado.

Grateful acknowledgment is made to the following persons for permission to reprint their own poems or other poems of which they control the copyright: S. Omar Barker, Walter S. Campbell, Kathleen C. Chapman, Vesta Pierce Crawford, Daisy L. Detrick, Thomas Hornsby Ferril, Ann Woodbury Hafen, Peter H. Holme, Sadie Howard Johnson, Gene Lindberg, Nellie Burget Miller, Arthur W. Monroe, John G. Neihardt, Clyde Robertson, Lilian White Spencer, and Alan Swallow.

The following publishers, also, kindly gave permission to reprint: Houghton Mifflin Company, the selection by Stanley Vestal; the Macmillan Company, the selection by John G. Neihardt; and Yale University Press, the selection by Thomas Hornsby Ferril. Due credit for these permissions and for those referred to in the preceding paragraph will be found included in the bibliographical notes following each poem in the anthology. The editor is deeply conscious of his obligation to all of the poets, living or dead, represented in this collection and hopes that the book will add to their honor.

Grateful acknowledgment, also, is made for assistance provided from The Research Fund of the University of Denver during the preparation of this anthology.

CONTENTS

A POETIC VERSION OF THE OLD WEST

Although modern poetic standards and techniques are quite different from those of our pioneering ancestors in the Rocky Mountain West, we can still enjoy many of the poems that they produced or that were written about them if we look for the values that these poems still possess. During the last decades of the nineteenth century and the early decades of the twentieth, old-time western events, characters, scenes, and attitudes were portrayed by hundreds of local poets, western newspaper versifiers, and other nearly forgotten authors. Dozens of collections, now gathering dust, were published by obscure presses, often at the poet's expense, for distribution to sympathetic friends and relatives. The approach was usually romantic and the poetic forms conventional; but the spirit of another era and the customs of a now-vanished way of life are preserved for us in the best of these writings. A few modern western poets have added to this store by their imaginative re-creations. Even if we read some of the older poems with a smile, because of their crudity or their shameless sentimentalism, we should remember that they reflect the taste of an earlier generation and that they express—often unconsciously—attitudes that are a vital part of the western tradition and myth.

The selections contained in this anthology are from the Rocky Mountain region. They treat Rocky Mountain subject matter; they are, for the most part, by poets who lived in the Rockies; and many of them were printed in Colorado or other Rocky Mountain states. Some of the authors attained the distinction of having New York or Boston publishers, but that fact does not insure that their works have greater interest for us today than do the anonymous verses that appeared in some western newspaper or magazine. In fact, the chief purpose of this collection is to rescue from oblivion a hundred or more poems that only a few modern readers know and to make them easily available. These poems do not excell in aesthetic appeal, but they are fun to read; and they are a part of our western cultural heritage even though we have neglected them.

Much of the poetry written in the Rocky Mountain West is deservedly forgotten. Too often it was composed by those who had nothing to say, who echoed the platitudes of popular Victorian versifiers, who used conventional topics and supposedly poetic language. The books by such mistakenly ambitious souls are not much different

9

from those by would-be but inadequate poets to be found in any other time and place. They are imitative and flat.

All such works were dusted off and scanned, usually in vain, by the present editor in his search for still-living verse that would contribute to a poetic portrait of the Old West. Fortunately, the Bargain Bookstore and the Bookery, in Denver, and the special collections of western literature in the Denver Public Library and the library of the State Historical Society of Colorado yielded many other volumes from each of which a poem or two could be culled worth rereading and reprinting in an anthology. From such books and from other widely scattered sources, such as newspapers and magazines, the present volume has been assembled.

Many good poets of the Rocky Mountain region are not represented in this anthology because their work does not treat specifically western themes. Some of the poets who have given permission to reprint would, no doubt, have chosen other selections of perhaps greater artistic merit or of a more representative nature than the ones that I preferred because of the purpose of the book. No collection can be exhaustive; but this one, it is hoped, will provide at least a generous sampling of the diverse poems that have attempted to portray the Old West.

June 1, 1951

Levette J. Davidson
University of Denver

I

THE LURE OF GOLD

THE GOLD SEEKER'S SONG

Anonymous

This song of great expectations, published in Mark Twain's hometown newspaper, expresses much of the innocent optimism which characterized the Argonauts in the spring of '59, when the Pike's Peak gold rush was at its height.

Take up the oxen, boys, and harness up the mules;
Pack away provisions and bring along the tools;
The pick and the shovel, and a pan that won't leak;
And we'll start for the gold mines. Hurrah for the Peak!

Then farewell to sweethearts, and farewell to wives,
And farewell to children, the joy of our lives;
We're bound for the Far West, the yellow dust to seek,
And as we march along we'll shout, "Hurrah for Pike's Peak!"

Then crack your whips, my jolly boys, we'll leave our homes behind,
And many lovely scenes that we'll often call to mind,
But we'll keep a merry heart, and we'll steer for Cherry creek;
For we're bound to hunt the yellow dust—Hurrah for Pike's Peak!

We'll cross the bold Missouri, and we'll steer for the west,
And we'll take the road we think is the shortest and the best;
We'll travel o'er the plains, where the wind is blowing bleak,
And the sandy wastes shall echo with — "Hurrah for Pike's Peak!"

We'll sit around the campfires when all our work is done,
And sing our song, and crack our jokes, and have our share of fun;
And when we're tired of jokes and song, our blankets we will seek,
To dream of friends, and home, and gold. Hurrah for Pike's Peak!

Then ho! for the mountain, where the yellow dust is found,
Where the grizzly bear, and the buffalo, and antelope abound;
We'll gather up the dust along the golden creek,
And make our "pile," and start for home. Hurrah for Pike's Peak!

From the *Hannibal* [Mo.] *Messenger*, April 28, 1859.

SONG FOR THE PIKE'S PEAKER

By "Syntax"

Optimism about finding gold continued in 1859 until the weather "closed in," as strikes were made near Clear Creek and in Boulder Canyon, Colorado; but an anonymous satirist questioned the use to which the gold might be put.

Ho! for Pike's Peak, where gold is found;
The shining dust is in the ground.
Where sands sparkle with precious ore,
The creeks are full, What need we more?

Ho! Ho! for the mountains ages old,
That lift their heads so grand and bold;
Their foreheads up in air so high,
They seem to press against the sky.

Ho! for their crests so gray and rough,
Their bosoms are surely rich enough,
With brilliant gold, more than all
E'er dug or seen since Adam's fall.

Ho! for the rivers and the rills,
Whose source is in those mighty hills
And sands are gold and costly stones;
Ho! for those lofty mountain cones.

Gold buys influence, honor, station,
Rules the powers of the nation
In all its branches, and asserts
Sovereign sway as its deserts.

Gets the Senator and his vote,
Gives the editor his keynote,
Rules the parson, makes him speak,
Lightly of sin done through the week,

Buys the judge, dictates the law,
Saves the wretch from hangman's claw,

14

Makes the ruffian an abject slave,
To rob, to murder, or to save.

Ho! away and our wagons fill,
With precious metal from the hill
Get this wand of mighty power,
The Pike's Peaker's golden dower.

Ho! let's away ere break of day
Until the mountain's stay our way,
And with sluice, shovel and pick,
Fill our coffers mighty quick.

Reprinted from the *Leavenworth* [Kansas] *Dispatch* in the *Rocky
Mountain Gold Reporter and Mountain City Herald,* Mountain
City, Colorado, September 10, 1859.

THE PIKE'S PEAKERS

By Lawrence N. Greenleaf

Early realism still found Colorado's gold seekers heroic and
romantic, if tough. Puns are common to humorous and satiric verse
of the period, as with Lawrence N. Greenleaf, "Peter Punever," who
in *King Sham* (1868) made himself the laureate of "the Pike's Peak
excitement." *King Sham* includes the following "anonymous" newspaper contribution, in revised and expanded form.

In '59 Pike's Peakers were a sight
To make a city dame turn ghastly white.
The chaps who roughed it coming 'cross the plains
In dress displayed no very 'tic'lar pains;
Long bushy hair upon their shoulders lay,
Their grizzly beards unshorn for many a day.
"Biled shirts" gave place to "hickory," plaid, or patch,
While graybacks brought the wearers to the scratch.
Stripes down their breeches looked uncommon queer,
A buckskin patch conspicuous in the rear.
Spectres, say you? Pro-spectors were the trumps
Who, delving in the mines, first found the lumps;

15

To them a tribute would I gladly pay.
Who "made the riffle" at an early day,
And set to work, though adverse tales were told,
And turned the scales with glittering scales of gold.
The Desperado was a savage cuss,
Eager to breed a row, or raise a muss,
Who snuffed afar the symptoms of a fight,
And drew his "Nivy" or his "Bowie" bright,
And always made it his exclusive "biz"
To mingle in a crowd and "let 'er whiz";
To shoot at random was a heap of fun,
Rare sport to see his victim's life-blood run!
On him at last the tables swift were turned;
A wholesome lesson to his cost he learned.
The "vigys" pointed to an empty saddle,
And gave him just ten minutes to skedaddle.

From the *Rocky Mountain News,* Denver, May 31, 1862.

A HIT AT THE TIMES

By A. O. McGrew

"Root hog, or die," the stirring song of the gold seekers, furnished
the pattern for many a parody commenting upon conditions in the
mining regions. A. O. McGrew is reported to have presented the
following at Denver's first Christmas celebration, in 1858. Since no
newspapers had yet appeared in the Cherry Creek diggings, the
poem was sent back to Omaha for publication.

Way out upon the Platte, near Pike's Peak we were told
There by a little digging, we could get a pile of gold,
So we bundled up our duds, resolved at least to try
And tempt old Madam Fortune, root hog, or die.

So we traveled across the country, and we got upon the ground,
But cold weather was ahead, the first thing we found.
We built our shanties on the ground, resolved in spring to try,
To gather up the dust and slugs, root hog, or die.

Speculation is the fashion even at this early stage,
And corner lots and big hotels appear to be the rage,
The emigration's bound to come, and to greet them we will try,
Big pig, little pig, root hog, or die.

Let shouts resound, the cup pass 'round, we all came for gold,
The politicians are all gas, the speculators sold,
The "scads" are all we want, and to get them we will try,
Big pig, little pig, root hog, or die.

Surveyors now are at their work, laying off the towns,
And some will be of low degree, and some of high renown.
They don't care a jot nor tittle who do buy
The corner lots, or any lots, root hog, or die.

The doctors are among us, you can find them where you will,
They say their trade it is to cure, I say it is to kill;
They'll dose you, and they'll physic you, until they make you sigh,
And their powders and their lotions make you root hog, or die.

The next in turn comes Lawyers, a precious set are they;
In the public dairy they drink the milk, their clients drink the whey.
A cunning set these fellows are; they'll sap you 'till you're dry,
And never leave you 'till you have to root hog, or die.

A Preacher, now is all we want, to make us all do good;
But at present, there's no lack of *spiritual* food,
The kind that I refer to, will make you laugh or cry,
And its real name is Taos, root hog, or die.

I have finished now my song, or, if you please, my ditty;
And that it was not shorter, is about the only pity.
And now, that I have had my say, don't say I've told a lie;
For the subject I've touched, will make us root hog, or die.

From the *Omaha Times,* February 17, 1859.

IN THE SUMMER OF SIXTY

Anonymous

The race for gold was ruthless, and the camps were full of "bunco-steerers." The following reports a not infrequent occurrence.

In the summer of sixty as you very well know
The excitement at Pike's Peak was then all the go;
Many went there with fortunes and spent what they had
And came back flat-busted and looking quite sad.

'Twas then I heard farming was a very fine branch,
So I spent most of my money in buying a ranch,
And when I got to it with sorrow and shame
I found a big miner had jumped my fine claim.

So I bought a revolver and swore I'd lay low
The very next fellow that treated me so;
I then went to Denver and cut quite a dash
And took extra pains to show off my cash.

With a fine span of horses, my wife by my side,
I drove through the streets with my hat on one side;
As we were agoin' past the old "Denver Hall"
Sweet music came out that did charm us all.

Says I, "Let's go in and see what's the muss
For I feel right now like having a fuss."
There were tables strung over the hall,
Some was a-whirling a wheel with a ball.

Some playin' cards and some shakin' dice
And lots of half dollars that looked very nice;
I finally strayed to a table at last
Where all the poor suckers did seem to stick fast.

And there stood a man with cards in his hand,
And these were the words which he did command,
"Now, gents, the winning card is the ace,
I guess you will know it if I show you its face."

One corner turned down, it's plain to be seen,
I looked at that fellow and thought he was green,
Yes I looked at that feller and thought he was green,
One corner turned down, 'twas so plain to be seen.

So I bet all my money and lo and behold!
'Twas a tray-spot of clubs and he took all my gold.
Then I went home and crawled into bed
And the divil a word to my wife ever said.

'Twas early next morning I felt for my purse
Biting my lips to keep down a curse;
Yes, 'twas early next morning as the sun did rise
You might have seen with your two blessed eyes,

In an ox wagon, 'twas me and my wife
Goin' down the Platte river for death or for life.

From Louise Pound, editor, *American Ballads and Songs* (New York: Charles Scribner's Sons, 1922), pp. 189-190.

SOLILOQUY OF THE RETURNED GOLD ADVENTURER

By "Syntax"

To many, the Pike's Peak rush seemed a hoax. D. C. Oakes, one of the "discoverers," was hanged in effigy, and Horace Greeley was reviled for his optimistic appraisal of western opportunity. The "go-backs" were numerous.

Been to Pike's Peak, lost all my dimes,
And for a week had "darn'd hard times"
Hunting for gold, 'mong rocks and hills,
Catching a cold, the fever and chills.
Got mighty sick — felt very sad,
Stung to the quick, times were so bad;
Money all spent, worn out my shoes,
Clothing all rent — I had the blues:
Got in the lurch — my spirits down,

Gave up the search, came back to town,
Footsore, weary, hungry, spleeny,
Heartsick, dreary, and ....greeny
To leave mother, a pleasant home,
And a dear brother, away to roam,
'Mong mountains rough, for golden ore:
I've had enough and nevermore
From mother's side, westward to stray,
What e're betide there will I stay
Under her care; plenty to eat,
Clothing to wear that can't be beat:
Broadcloth, doeskin, bootees from bossy,
Beaver and satin, gloves soft and glossy:
I'll sport some curls, moustache and canes,
Loved by the girls, I'll take some pains
To cut a swell, be very nice,
Can do it well, just like a mice;
I'll cut a dash, take rustic down,
Spend mother's cash, surprise the town,
Make time my toy, ne'er have a care,
Be a wild boy and beau the fair.

Reprinted from the Leavenworth, Kansas, *Evening Dispatch* in the *Rocky Mountain News*, Denver, October 20, 1859.

ME AND PRUNES

By Rupe Sherwood

Lonely prospectors, accompanied only by their burros, persevered in the search for El Dorado, penetrating even the most remote mountains. When the gold miners went underground, they took along the faithful little beasts of burden. A monument in Fairplay, Colorado, reads as follows: "Prunes — A Burro. 1867-1930. Fairplay — Alma—All Mines in this District." In accordance with his request, the author of the following tribute was cremated upon his death, in 1931, and his ashes were buried near the monument.

So poor old Prunes has cashed in — Too bad. Still, in a way
    I'm glad the old boy's eased off and is calling it a day.

I'm going to miss him scand'lous; the world won't seem the same
　　Not having him a-standin' here hee-hawing in the game.
We've sure drawed cards together aplenty: Prunes and me;
　　We've bucked the play in every way the cards was dealt to we:
Sometimes we filled our hands and won — so seldom 'twas a joke —
　　Most often we just bob-tail flushed and wound up stony broke.
But no matter if we win or lose, old Prunes hee-hawed the same;
　　The trails were all alike to him: it all was in the game
We played with fortune. Come the breaks our way or plumb 'gainst
　　　us
　　Old Prunes just toted fair and stuck 'thout making ary fuss.
When grub was plenty, grass was long, and trails was smooth he took
　　His share and share alike with me. If things went scant he shook
His head and laffed: "Hee-haw — Hee-haw!" The philosophic cuss!
　　And dined on greasy gunnysacks an' bacon rinds — an' wuss.
I've prospected in company with every kind of man
　　That ever hit these hills. Sometimes I'd meet with one who'd pan
Out fairly good; but mostly they was allus lookin' out
　　For Number One. I reckon you know what I'm talking 'bout.
I've throwed in with 'em—every race an' breed an' color, too—
　　An' found 'em all just lackin' of some one thing—maybe two.
Some had no guts; some had no sense; some wasn't honest; so
　　Not one of them could average up with Prunes, my old burro.
For Prunes was faithful, honest, an' he never tried to shirk
　　From doin' of his bit, no matter how damned hard the work.
And he didn't grouch and grumble when the eats was kinda short:
　　He took all things just as they come. Old Prunes was a good
　　　sport!
An' I don't think he delib'rately laid down on me when come
　　His time to peter out and hit the trail for Jackass Home.
But I'm kinda peeved to think he's goin' it upon his own
　　An' leavin' me behind to play the deal out all alone.
I'm not much on religion; and sometimes I've a doubt
　　About this "Immortality" sky-pilots rave about.
But I'm gamblin' if there be another life after this one
　　It won't be just restricted to the things called man alone.
But every thing now livin' will surely live again—
　　(I know a hundred that deserves to, more than most of men)
An' if they do, why, sure as shootin' mongst those heavenly tunes
　　I'll betcha fifty bucks we'll hear the "Hee-haw" of old Prunes.

21

Maybe the preachers got it right. I hope they have! I'd like
    Along with Prunes, among those golden fields to take a hike.
We'd sure find pay dirt if it's there. You betcher life on that.
    For Prunes an' me knows values when we see them — that is flat!
An' if, belike, they shouldn't reckon us just good enough
    To trail 'round with the gang up there, and go to treat us rough
An' slide us down the chute to where no icy moss festoons,
    We'd prospect there for sulphurets — and find 'em, too. Hey,
        Prunes?

From a four page announcement of the death of Rupert M. Sherwood
printed by the *Summit County Journal* of Breckenridge, Colorado.

THE BURRO

By The Reverend J. J. Gibbons

    Humorous but heart-felt is the tribute to the burro that the
Reverend J. J. Gibbons wrote after a score of years as missionary in the
San Juan country of southwestern Colorado. Without the burro,
pioneering in the mining region of the Rockies before the days of
jeeps and trucks would have been almost impossible.

    When Adam named in days of old,
    The bird and beast and every fold,
    He gave to each its proper class,
    And well defined the gentle ass,
    His ears made long, inclined to flap,
    Down his shoulders is nature's strap.
    Thus marked, he went o'er the world wide,
    To help us all by easy stride.
    Docile, humble, of low degree,
    Destined ever a slave to be,
    He took his place when time began,
    And since has been the friend of man.
    From Eastern climes he made his way,
    Where his'try marks his longest stay,
    And to the West, o'er ocean's main,
    With Adam's sons he swelled the train;
    But man, like ever-shifting fame,

Resolved to change the donkey's name.
Away on mountain, far from throng,
The sound he made, man called a song.
So, moved by notes, most deem scary,
Some dub him now the new canary.

From early morn to close of day,
He sings his song the same old way.
His voice is harsh, a choking roar,
And fills the mind with thoughts of gore.
His notes, — one short, with two quite long,
Contain the burden of his song.
At midnight hour when nature rests,
His crooning bray breaks out the best,
And o'er the crags and passes bleak,
His voice resounds in dismal shriek,
And some will cry when they are airy,
That "He's a bird — a true canary."
The burro is his Spanish name
And bearing it he rose to fame;
For up and down 'neath driver's wrath,
He climbs with load on narrow path,
Where slipp'ry trails and icy slate
Precipitate him to his fate.
Plodding along at break of day,
So, year by year he makes his way,
Loaded heavy in mountain dust,
In winter's snows, and clouds that burst.
Keeping his pace in sun and rain,
He creeps along a mountain train.
In hunger, they say, oft he can,
When all is gone, consume a can.
Bridles, saddles and boxes too;
He'll also eat a soleless shoe,
Flour and coffee, bacon and ham,
He looks upon, as we do jam.
Butter and cheese left in the shade,
Will disappear on his parade.
Trousers and shirts, in time of need,
Make him a meal for sharpest greed.

But of the things beyond his skill
Are iron hammer, miner's drill.
Around the camp he always goes
Striking at dogs and kindred foes,
Braying aloud with great delight
When hay abounds and grain's in sight;
Sometimes limping from saddle sore
Dug in his back by sacks of ore.
Taking ills like a patient man,
He spends his time the best he can,
Careless of wounds and battered feet,
Stumbling along the stony street;
Or, standing meek, with load or pack,
Eats the hay from his partner's back.

When flowers bloom and days are fine,
The burro keeps in better line.
When roads are good, and grass is long,
With stomach full he pegs along;
And o'er the hills and craggy walls
He carries nymphs from Vassar's halls.
'Neath Harvard's sports, or men from Yale,
The same old wag is in his tail.
The schoolmarms, too, both young and old,
Ride him up through the mountains bold.
His faithfulness should prompt us so
To treat him well where e'er we go.
A friend to all on dreary pass,
Most useful is the modest ass.

J. J. Gibbons, *In the San Juan, Colorado* (Chicago: Calumet Book and Engraving Co., 1898), pp. 117-119.

SONG

By Scott Judy and "Doc" Hammond

The mountain gold camps were often deserted during the heavy snows. Those who "holed in" for the winter had plenty of time to compose local poems, such as the following. It was made up in 1880, in the present camp of Whitepine, by two prospectors.

We came to Tamichi in 1880
Looking for mineral all the hills o'er,
We travelled the valleys and climbed the steep mountains
Till our feet were all blistered, our legs were all sore.

We packed from the wagons the crooked trail over;
We held a big meeting and voted free roads;
But Boone and Jess Davis they downed old Judge Tucker,
And now all us boys will have to pay toll.

We lived on sow-belly, baked beans and strong coffee;
We done our own cooking and washed our own clothes;
We polished the drill like any old-timer,
And put on the rocks our good honest blows.

The mail to our camp, it came on the jack-train;
Oh jolly Tom Allen, the chief engineer,
He carried our chuck for chick and the miners,
And to the Windsor brought moonshine and beer.

We drank at Ed Dyart's, the solid old duffer,
We'd wink and say, "Ed, mark her down on the slate,
When we strike it we'll ante and then you can rub it."
He'd smile and say, "Boys, you are rather too late."

There is Thomas O'Riley, who lives in Creede City,
A jolly old bummer, you can bet your last cent;
For punishing booze, he can beat any baby;
They say that for women, Old Tom is hell bent.

There's old Judge and Ben, who live in the Buckhorn,
They struck a big thing in their own Sleepy Pet;

They were solid for Hancock 'til they heard from Indiana.
"We've struck it!" says the Judge, — "Won't you take something wet?"

Oh, yes, there's another; you may count him a winner;
'Tis said that they struck him while boring for oil;
He runs the Strawberry and works on the Free Road;
'Tis nobody else but our own Andy Boil.

Goodby, old pards, we are going to leave you:
The blanket's rolled up, and the pick's laid away;
We are going Home, to eat Christmas turkey,
We'll meet you again, when the snow melts away.

From *Interviews* collected by workers on the Colorado Writers' Program of the WPA for the State Historical Society of Colorado. Margaret Flick, Gunnison County, March 15, 1934.

THE OL' JINNY MINE

By Daisy L. Detrick

Without benefit of electronic equipment, the early prospectors made their strikes with strange and lucky aids, and named their mines after tin cups or jack and jenny asses.

Yep, gold's where you find it. You betcha that's true.
This happened at Alma 'long 'bout eighty-two.
Jim Haley'd been prospectin' year after year
From springtime to snow, and it seemed sorta queer
That a gambler from Leadville would grubstake Ol' Jim,
To make one more try with the chances so slim,
But he did. Well, the weather warmed up some in May
And Jim headed Jinny up Mosquito Pass way.

Say, you ARE a tenderfoot now fer a fac'.
Why, a Jinny's a lazy, low-down lady Jack;
A burro to tote your bed-blankets and jeans,
Your sow-belly, coffee, flour, baccy and beans,
Your coffee-pot, fryin' pan—Lord knows what more,
And a diamond hitch holds 'em behind and before.

Jim thought Dead Horse Gulch was the likeliest place
But he hunted for weeks without findin' a trace
Of the gold-bearin' quartz vein he hoped would crop out
Like the ones folks in Leadville had gone wild about.
Ol' Jim was sure blue, fer it soon would be fall
And he and the gambler had nothin' at all.
He prodded the Jinny across a rock ledge;
She crowded him over too close to the edge
That was crumblin' because of the frost and the snow
And over they rolled to the slope down below,
Where a clump of pines stopped 'em; but they started a slide
That roared down the mountain a hundred yards wide!
Not a bone did Jim break, but his head got a rap
That put him to sleep fer a sizeable nap!
He woke with a thump in his grizzled ol' head,
So stiff and so sore that he wished he was dead.
He heard a long bray, and there on the trail
Was Jinny jes lazily switchin' her tail
With nary a pack. Her long ears flapped at Jim
Like the hull thing was funny and the joke was on him.
It sure made Jim mad. He reached out fer a rock;
He'd give that wench Jinny one gosh awful sock
He bet she'd remember! But the rock in his hand
Never stung Jinny's rump as Ol' Jim had planned.
In the sunshine the quartz shone with webs of free gold!
Those two had uncovered the vein when they rolled
Down the mountain and started the slide. Jinny knew
And *pushed* him, Jim said. I won't say it ain't true.
Fer gold's where you find it. If a burro helps — fine!
They dug out a lot from that Ol' Jinny mine.

Printed by special permission of the author from an unpublished manuscript.

THE LITTLE JOHNNY MINE

By Daisy L. Detrick

Molly Tobin, wife of Johnny Brown, became famous, in the *Titanic* disaster, as "The Unsinkable Mrs. Brown." Here is one version of the story of Johnny Brown's first strike in Leadville, Colorado, written by a Denver poet.

Old Leadville was booming in eighty-eight;
Molly Tobin was lured by its golden bait.
She set up her tent where one street showed a gap
And lettered a sign high above the tent flap.
The prospectors brought her their laundry and mending
And Johnny came too, just as Fate was intending.
No Adonis was Johnny; red-haired and uncouth,
Full twenty years past the first flush of his youth,
But "a way with the women." Such a strange thing is life.
Three weeks from that day he made Molly his wife!

Now the lank buckskin bag in his faded old jeans
Contained scarcely "dust" for their bacon and beans,
There were two happy months playing poverty's game,
Then Johnny discovered pay dirt on his claim.
It assayed. The experts confirmed it real gold.
Three hundred grand offered — a fortune! He sold.
"It's got to be cash though," was Johnny's demand,
"Three hundred news bills to put in the hand
Of the purtiest gal in this hull ding danged town,
An' that gal is my wife, Mrs. Johnny J. Brown."

He clutched the plump roll, then rushed home to find Molly;
Kicked open the door; bellowed, "Rich, rich, by golly!
Got t' celebrate some at the SADDLE ROCK BAR."
Little Molly was dazed, but she first tucked away
In the kitchen stove oven (now cold for the day)
The bewildering roll. Then to calm her poor head
She blew out the light and slipped into her bed.

Near dawn a friend opened the rear shanty door
And eased Johnny down to the bare kitchen floor.
Such a cold place to sleep! It would rouse Johnny's ire
To disturb his young wife, so — he built a good fire!
The crackling grew louder and Molly awoke
But the three hundred "grand" had all gone up in smoke!
Soon her wails wakened Johnny. She sobbed out the tale,
But he laughed. "No use bawlin' 'bout burnin' the kale.
I'll find yo' some more. Here, we've got the stove hot,
Let's boil up some coffee right strong in the pot."

Now the very next day Johnny staked out a claim;
It was just for luck, maybe, he gave it HIS name.
The world long has known of that fabulous "find,"
The incredible gold vein that later was mined.
To the day of his death with an oath Johnny'd swear
That a certain FIRE made him a danged millionaire!

Printed by special permission of the author from an unpublished manuscript.

THE BALLAD OF CHICKEN BILL

By F. E. Vaughn

An old prospector called Chicken Bill sold the famous H. A. W. Tabor a shaft salted with ore from Tabor's own Little Pittsburg mine at Leadville, Colorado. Although Tabor soon learned that he had been duped, he put men to work on his new property. His "Midas touch" worked again; he hit the great Chrysolite lode and turned a hoax into a bonanza.

Of course you have read of the wicked ways
Of Leadville town in the early days,
Of the "killers" and "grafters" who lived here when
The place was peopled by gambling men,
    When it cost a fortune to eat and sleep,
    When life and morals both were cheap,
    And one owned all one could get — and keep.

Men who had sifted the golden sands
From the mountain peaks of many lands;
Capitalist, criminal, tenderfoot, tramp,
All drifted into the silver camp.
　　By luck, design, or by God's will,
　　There lived in a shack on Fryer hill,
　　A prospector known as Chicken Bill.

This was 'way back in seventy-nine,
When every claim was a paying mine,
When money and suckers both were thick,
And prospects sold without stroke of pick.
　　Then the boys and the camp were thorobred,
　　One got drunk and painted the other red,
　　And maybe wound up half filled with lead.

This Chicken Bill was a queer old cuss,
Who worked away without making a fuss,
Sinking a hole into Fryer hill
With pick and shovel and iron will,
　　But he had a mild and simple look
　　And a face you could read like an open book—
　　With a handshake that couldn't be mistook.

Bill's shaft was down some seventy feet
In a wash formation, hard to beat
With one man twisting an old "armstrong,"
His work was hard and his hours were long;
　　When Hook and Rische and Tabor found
　　The Pittsburg bonanza lying around,
　　With dollars almost on top of the ground.

Old Chicken Bill went down to look
At the prospect opened by Rische and Hook,
Chloride ore of the finest kind,
And every seam was "Shamrock" lined.
　　He looked it over and opened his eyes
　　At sight of the dazzling silver prize,
　　But he said nothing — for Bill was wise.

That night as he lay in his lonely bed
On the old hill side in the dirt thatched shed
A brilliant thought flashed through his brain
Which he sifted over and over again.
> For Bill had learned in by gone days
> Sundry and various crooked ways,
> And he said: "Everything is right that pays."

Three shifts were working on the jump
Piling the ore on the Pittsburg dump,
Thousands of dollars were lying there,
And millons more below to spare.
> Bill took a few sacks of Pittsburg ore,
> Just what he needed — not a bit more —
> It was never missed from the bountiful store.

Things were "doin'" 'round his shaft that night
In the pallid glare of the old moon's light,
And when he had finished he softly laughed —
There was lots of ore in old Bill's shaft—
> Ore on the dump and lying around,
> Ore like the Little Pittsburg found,
> Ore on top and underground.

Next day when Tabor came on the hill
He went to see old Chicken Bill,
He found him sitting on the dump
With a microscope on a d——d rich lump.
> Now Tabor didn't "pike" or "stall,"
> And it was a big bluff he wouldn't call,
> So he bought out Chicken Bill — that's all.

Nine hundred dollars, so they say.
Was the price that Tabor had to pay
(Some fellers may dispute that same),
For a quit-claim deed to the Matchless claim.
> Out of the country went Chicken Bill,
> Leaving Tabor with mighty good will —
> And the "wash" hole up in Fryer hill.

Some stories have sequels, so they say,
And when Tabor went up the following day
He wasn't feeling so very fine,
For he found he had purchased a "salted" mine.
 Salted, as I have said before,
 From the Pittsburg dump with Tabor's ore —
 'Twas enough to make a man feel sore.

But Tabor had money, and Tabor had sand,
With a world of faith at his command,
He put that shaft down ten feet more,
And this time Tabor got the ore!
 A million dollars was what he made,
 After the trick the smooth man played —
 That was because he always "STAYED!"

Now just a few words about Tabor's ways
From one who knew him in bygone days:
His heart and bank account were big,
He stood by his friends and didn't renege.
 He was the man who won renown
 By making a city of Denver town,
 Before the parasites threw him down.

Times have changed — hair turned gray,
And many old-timers have passed away.
The bad man has gone to his final rest
From the silver camp of the golden west.
 Exit Tabor and Chicken Bill,
 But over there is Fryer hill
 Quietly producing millions still.

F. E. Vaughn, *The Spirit of Leadville in Verse* (n.p., 1929).

MISTRESS OF THE MATCHLESS MINE

By Clyde Robertson

After Tabor and his fortune were gone, his wife went back to "cabin life" in a shack near the Matchless Mine, which on his death-bed Tabor had instructed her not to sell, saying, "Hold on to the Matchless."

A blinding spot burned on the snow
Where no spot was; an undertow
Where no sea ran, tugged at her feet —
A tom-tom drummed a maddening beat
Into her ears, though not a sound
Fretted the air or frozen ground.

Once, she turned with a last farewell
To the Camp below: "The years will tell
Who were the great and who the small!
He was greater than you all:
The ore runs rich and the veins run wide
In the golden hills on the Great Divide:
Wide and rich as the gold veins run,
He left his trail in the Western sun."

The spot on the snow grew red as blood
And she seemed to wade through a freezing flood.
She would reach the shack. She would bar the door
On the jeering world as she'd done before.
She clutched the coin in her withered hand
With fingers stiff as a steely band.
When she was dead, and they found here there,
They would find she still had gold to spare.

Burned in her brain were the words he said,
He, greater than all, now long since dead:
"Swear by the saints you always will
Stay with the lode on Fryer Hill.
Stick like the roots of an old jack pine,
Never give up the Matchless Mine."

It had come to mean, as the years grew old,
Something more than a hill of gold;
It was not a mountain, it was a man!
Glorified in a granite span.
It was not a mine, but flesh and blood
Caught in the swirl of a golden flood!

Her fumbling fingers forced the latch
And coaxed a spark from a sodden match.
Cold as the icy clutch of doom,
The black damp filtered through the room.
But the red spot followed and burned the wall
Till the bare room blazed like a banquet hall;
And there, in the golden circle, shone
The glamorous scenes she once had known.
The tattered quilt, in her dark death sweat,
Became a satin coverlet.
She was again the courted queen
And he a man of kingly mien.

A wildcat wailed on Fryer Hill,
A woman sighed, then all was still.
The last coin of her golden store
Fell from her hand; across the floor
A pilfering pack rat slyly stole
And dragged it off to his robber hole.
Still the faithful fingers cling
To a rosary — a knotted string —
A knotted string where a prayer still lingers,
Clasped in the quiet, calloused fingers.

A gutted candle, black in the socket,
A man's face, in a tarnished locket,
A lean rat, making ready to leap,
A woman, open-eyed, asleep.

She who could write with a scholar's pen,
She who could speak with the best of men,
She who had shone like a jeweled plaque —
Dead with her dreams in a mountain shack.

Holy Mother, grant her peace,
Grant an uncontested lease
Beyond the Great Divide's dark line
To the Mistress of the Matchless Mine.

Clyde Robertson, *The Yellow Witch* (New York: Loker Raley, 1940), pp. 13-15. Reprinted by special permission of the author.

THE YELLOW WITCH OF CARIBOU

By Clyde Robertson

A modern regional poet invents a legend of "the lure of gold," to portray by personification an age-old situation, illustrated countless times in the stories of Rocky Mountain prospectors.

The hills are high in Caribou—
The air is clear, the skies are blue;
But where a black ledge seams the ground
The yellow witch's tracks are found,
And men grow drunk with ravishment
Once they have caught the witch's scent.

The aspens on the mountain side
Were green when Carlo brought his bride,
The cherry-cheeked Selina, to
The haunted hills of Caribou.

"You better take your man and go,"
The old wives warned, "before the snow.
The yellow witch hides in these hills,
And gets our men against their wills."

Selina shook her bold, black head.
"My Carlo will not leave my bed
And hammer on a speckled door
A-huntin' for a yellow whore.
He's signed up with the sawmill crew,
He's safe enough in Caribou.

"Who minds the talk of wrinkled crones,
Their skin a-stickin' to their bones,
Their men folks might go trailin' round
A-chasin' witch tracks in the ground;
But my man's *mine!* I'm not afraid
I'll lose him to a stealin' jade."

"Child, we were all the same as you,
When we were brought to Caribou.
We know, as only old wives can,
The curse of havin' half a man.
We know the end of these old tracks —
The blinded eyes — and broken backs."

But when the mountain side grew red
And pulsing as a wanton's bed
Young Carlo's eyes flamed with the fire
Of an unhallowed, mad desire.
Selina knew his passion meant
"Her man" had caught the witch's scent.

Before the first snow veiled the crest,
Like lace upon a woman's breast,
She saw him leave the sheltering mills
To roam among the siren hills.

But no man yet has come to know
Which way the yellow witch may go.
She burrows deep in porphyry rocks
And bars her trail with granite blocks.
So Carlo did, as all men do
That chase the witch of Caribou.

At last upon a sloping crest,
As rounded as a woman's breast,
Beneath a snow of winding lace,
He tracked her to her hiding place.
Here, in an evil blackened niche,
He mated with the yellow witch.

At dawn, Selina found him there
Strangled by a golden hair.

Clyde Robertson, *The Yellow Witch* (New York: Loker Raley, 1940),
pp. 78-79. Reprinted by special permission of the author.

THE SLIDE AT THE EMPIRE MINE

By Harriet L. Wason

Nothing held more terror for miners in the high country of
Colorado than the thundering roar of an unpredictable, almost un-
escapable snow mass. The incident described below seems to have
occurred on December 1, 1880, at Atlantic City, about six miles from
Empire on the Hot Sulphur Springs Road.

All day a steady snow had drifted down,
Hiding the restful hues of dun and brown
On friendly hill-side, and the slender trail,
That bound us world-ward. Did no spirit quail
At the appalling doom looming before us,
With the unsettled snow-mass trembling o'er us?

If any feared, none spoke; the laugh and jest
Rang out as clear, perhaps with added zest
And but that they who worked at night-shift stood
With outstretched palms, in half unwilling mood
To leave the fire, no outward sign betrayed
If any felt discouraged or dismayed.

The storm had lulled, but the insatiate wind
Trailed a pathetic, vengeful wail behind,
When the brave four took courage, shut the light
And genial glow out from the prying night.

Six yet remained, not one essayed to speak;
The silence broken by a stifled shriek
That blanched all lips, and every man upsprung;
Wide to the night the cabin door was flung.

A rude gust quenched our lamp, and darkness gave
To unknown ill the horror of the grave,
A whirring din, a roll like distant thunder,
On coming, as the hills were rent asunder,
And with hushed breath we each the other eyed,
Knowing we faced that awful thing, a slide!

Our world-ward trail was sheltered by a ledge,
(Rising on one side like a rocky hedge,)
That served for shielding some the cabin door,
And as a quaking mass went thundering o'er
Beyond the trail, leaving it bare and steep,
Into a yawning chasm fathoms deep,
Our unbound hearts leaped upward with a sigh—
For us the King of Terrors had passed by.

The shaft-house from the cabin lay some feet,
Barely five score: but every tempest beat
With cruel fury thro' a small ravine
Across the trail, wholly devoid of screen;
And quite lost now. Instinct our only guide,
We labored blindly and on either side
A comrade found. These both alive were saved,
The shaft-house walls were whole, the roof had caved
And buried two, quite dead, tho' barely cold —
A sight that cowed the bravest to behold.

Will Clark was but a lad, not yet eighteen,
We know some household darling he had been;
For he had gentle speech and dainty ways,
Appeared to yearn for our good will and praise,
The other, Jack Monroe, was the reverse:
He sandwiched every sentence with a curse,
Defiant seemed, alike of God and man,
To such extremes his daily actions ran;
Yet strange to say, his friendship for the youth
Was strong as death, and beautiful as truth.

We found his giant body wedged between
The splintered rafters; an effectual screen

38

From their sharp spears, shielding the tender frame
As oft his tongue had sheltered him from blame;
One great hand held the slender fingers close,
One couched the head in its last long repose,
And thus they sleep, our pitying hands provided,
Who living, loved, in death were not divided.

Harriet L. Wason, *Letters from Colorado* (Boston: Cupples **and** Hurd, 1887), pp. 154-156.

THE MINER

By Alfred Castner King

A blind bard of the Rockies fitted his sense of the miner's **plight** to the rhythms more complicated than those of Hood's *Song of the Shirt.*

> Clink! Clink! Clink!
> The song of the hammer and drill!
> At the sound of the whistle so shrill and clear,
> He must leave the wife and the children dear,
> In his cabin upon the hill.
> Clink! Clink! Clink!
> But the arms that deliver the sturdy stroke,
> Ere the shift is done, may be crushed or broke,
> Or the life may succumb to the gas and smoke,
> Which the underground caverns fill.

> Clink! Clink! Clink!
> The song of the hammer and drill!
> As he toils in the shaft, in the stope or raise,
> 'Mid dangers which lurk, but elude the gaze,
> His nerves with no terrors thrill.
> Clink! Clink! Clink!
> For the heart of the miner is strong and brave;
> Though the rocks may fall, and the shaft may cave
> And become his dungeon, if not his grave,
> He braves every thought of ill.

Clink! Clink! Clink!
The song of the hammer and drill!
But the heart which is beating in unison
With the steady stroke, e'er the shift is done,
    May be cold and forever still.
        Clink! Clink! Clink!
He may reap the harvest of danger sowed,
The hole which he drills he may never load,
For the powder may e'en in his hand explode,
    To mangle, if not to kill.

        Clink! Clink! Clink!
    The song of the hammer and drill!
Facing dangers more grim than the cannon's mouth;
Breathing poisons more foul than the swamps of the south
    In their tropical fens distill.
        Clink! Clink! Clink!
Thus the battle he fights for his daily bread;
Thus our gold and our silver, our iron and lead,
Cost us lives, as true as our blood is red,
    And probably always will.

Alfred Castner King, *Mountain Idylls and Other Poems* (Chicago:
Fleming H. Revell Co., 1901), pp. 46-47.

DRILLING MISSED HOLES

By Don Cameron, "Prospector"

According to a quotation from *The Leadville News Dispatch,*
1880, which serves as a preface to the volume from which the following is taken, " 'Prospector' is a typical '79 miner. His specialty is
satire. He writes whenever the spirit moves him." He seems to dis-
like the later days of imported day labor and of underground mining.

        There's a death-dealing custom,
            Abroad in the land,
        I can see by the verdicts
            On every hand.

No fires lit with coal oil
  Nor rushing the goals,
Are so fearfully fatal,
  As drilling missed holes.

When bosses are planning,
  Some trouble to meet
They fill up the mines,
  With some cheap tenderfeet.
And the juryman's mirth
  He can scarcely control
For he knows it's so easy
  To drill a missed hole.

The miners at Bullion
  Were out on a strike,
And they watched a performance
  They didn't quite like;
A chee-chako preparing
  To light his first charge,
His experience was small,
  But his confidence large —

He saw the crowd smiling,
  And cursed the whole lot,
And swore he knew all
  About firing a shot.
The boys said they noticed
  His fuse was too short,
But he lit it, they know,
  For they heard the report.
The tales were conflicting,
  The jury looked droll,
But they found the "Departed
  Had drilled a missed hole."

Last week at the quarry
  On Bessemer hill,
A Swede disappeared
  With a keg and a drill;

And the papers came out
  With a long rigmarole
'Neath a caption like this—
  "Miner drills the missed hole."

The Polander, Ryewhiski,
  Who worked on the grade,
Spit his fuse, but he missed
  And the work was delayed
'Til Mickey, the boss,
  In a terrible stew
Told Ryewhiski to
  Try it again P.D.Q.

The explosion was fearful,
  Excitement ran high,
While the smoke and a shower
  Of rocks, darkened the sky.
It was hard to tell what
  Had become of the Pole,
But the verdict was easy —
  He drilled a missed hole.

An Italian was seen
  Going into a drift
With a charge such as only
  A burro might lift.
On his hat were his candle
  And piece of capped fuse;
Yet some people expressed
  Great surprise at the news,

Of the crash which soon followed,
  And then on the street
It was learned the destruction
  Was almost complete.
The track was all twisted,
  The timbers all wrecked,
But signs of poor "Tony"
  Were hard to detect.

We found some old rags
    And a spoonful of brains,
The "Intelligent jury
    Who viewed the remains,"
In their kindness of heart,
    Did the poor wife console,
By finding her husband
    Had drilled a missed hole.

There are verdicts of "heart-failure,"
    "Apoplexy,"
"Temporary insanity,"
    "Felo de se,"
But juries find nothing
    So dear to their souls
As unanimous verdicts
    Of drilling missed holes.

Don Cameron, *Satire of a Prospector* (n.p., n.d.), pp. 9-11.

SONG OF THE LEADVILLE MINE BOSS

By Don Cameron, "Prospector"

Again the old "Prospector" satirizes the new order.

"Wake up! Wake up! you bloomin' lot
    O' loafers don't be shirkin'.
Remember you have only got
    Ten hours to do your work in.

"Come make these picks and shovels hum
    And don't the rag be chewing,
Three dollars is a tidy sum
    To pay for all you're doing.

"Rush! Lam these drill! you sons o' guns
    And fly with car and barrow,
Unless we get five hundred tons
    You'll all be sacked tomorrow.

"Don't forget the day is passed
      When you could 'take a taper'
You've got to travel mighty fast
      Or take your 'piece o' paper.'

"There was a time in Leadville when
      You found it easy labor;
When Leadville mines were owned by men
      Like Stevens, Wood and Tabor.

"But not content, you had to wreck
      Your prospects then by striking!
They gave it to you in the neck,
      Contrary to your liking.

"Those were the days when scheming jays
      High-handed things did carry,
But now we're on to all your plays
      And every thrust can parry.

"To strike a fast increasing pace
      Thenceforth has been your sentence,
'Tis mine — the modern boss' — place
      To bring you to repentence.

"You thought to make this camp — you fools —
      A place to loaf and feed in
We've changed all that — with pliant tools
      From Italy and Sweden.

"Step lively! Mike, my bloomin' duck,
      And keep that barrow waltzin'
Come! Chase yourself! and wheel that muck
      Away from Ollie Olson.

"Stand back! Old Leadville Pioneer;
      Your movements should be brisker
Before you seek employment here
      Go off and dye your whisker.

44

"The notion that a boss should judge
        A man by his ability
    Is busted! You must wear a badge
        And look of true humility.

"Giv'n speed of hound and strength of bull
        With humble mien of Jesus,
    You'd still require a social 'pull'
        E'er you could hope to please us!

"Hi! Hi there! Hurry up! O'Toole
        Get right up in the collar!
    I hope to see the day when you'll
        Be working for a dollar."

Don Cameron, *Satire of a Prospector* (n.p., n.d.), pp. 22-23.

CREEDE

By Cy Warman

One of the most quoted of all western poems, these two stanzas
have crystallized truth into legend. Creede, Colorado, developed
almost overnight and declined almost as rapidly.

            Here's a land where all are equal —
                Of high or lowly birth —
            A land where men make millions,
                Dug from the dreary earth.
            Here the meek and mild-eyed burro
                On mineral mountains feed —
            It's day all day, in the day-time,
                And there is no night in Creede.

            The cliffs are solid silver,
                With wond'rous wealth untold;
            And the beds of running rivers
                Are lined with glittering gold.

While the world is filled with sorrow,
    And hearts must break and bleed —
It's day all day in the day-time,
    And there is no night in Creede.

Cy Warman, *Mountain Melodies* (Denver, n.d.) , p. 10.

THE RISE AND FALL OF CREEDE

By Cy Warman

Warman's epitaph on the old Creede wild life is less well known, but filled with more historical detail and color.

A thousand burdened burros filled
    The narrow, winding, wriggling trail.
A hundred settlers came to build,
    Each day, new houses in the vale.
A hundred gamblers came to feed
    On these same settlers — this was Creede.

Slanting Annie, Gambler Joe
    And bad Bob Ford, Sapolio, —
Or Soapy Smith, as he was known, —
    Ran games peculiarly their own,
And everything was open wide,
    And men drank absinthe on the side.
        . . . . . .
And now the Faro Bank is closed,
    And Mr. Faro's gone away
To seek new fields, it is supposed, —
    More verdant fields. The gamblers say
The man who worked the shell and ball
    Has gone back to the Capitol.

The winter winds blow bleak and chill,
    The quaking, quivering aspen waves
About the summit of the hill—
    Above the unrecorded graves
Where halt, abandoned burros feed
    And coyotes call — and this is Creede.

46

Lone graves whose head-boards bear no name,
   Whose silent owners lived like brutes
And died as doggedly, — but game,
   And most of them died in their boots.
We mind among the unwrit names
   The man who murdered Jesse James.

We saw him murdered, saw him fall,
   And saw his mad assassin gloat
Above him. Heard his moans and all,
   And saw the shot holes in his throat,
And men moved on and gave no heed
   To life or death — and this is Creede.

Cy Warman, *Songs of Cy Warman* (Boston: Rand Avery Co.;
Toronto: McLeod & Allen, 1911), pp. 76-77.

THE GOLD SEEKERS

By Marion Muir Richardson

Poetic legend-making ties the miscellaneous fates of gold seekers
with the Indian's dispossession, which the treasure hunts had caused.

The dim stars wheeled above the frontier post,
The wolf was silent, and the wind was lost;
The fire roared upward, lighting with its flames
Four white men's faces and four strong young frames.
They told how deer were plenty, by the Blue
In upland forests, till a red man threw
In from the window ledge a stone that rolled
Straight to their feet, and it was glittering gold.
Mad with desire to find the parent vein
They parted; one went southward where the plain
Returns his fervor to the burning sun,
And he was found, before his search was done,
With shriveled fingers, digging in the sand,
And black lips pressed against the thirsting land—
No look of grace to mark him woman-born —
A thing of horror that the wolves had torn.

47

But one climbed higher, where the budding flower
Bends, in mid August, to the sharp snow shower,
Frost bitten and frost blinded, sheathed in ice,
Among the cold, white mountain-tops he lies.
The third, in luck, found fortune and a bride,
A dainty dame, white-handed, gentle-eyed,
Yet, woe for woman's truth, she brought him shame,
Ruin, regret, a life without an aim.
Still the fourth man is wandering on and on;
With eyes that seek the distance, or the dawn
Of some new day, in loneliness he goes
Through waste or crowd, he neither cares nor knows.
    Up and down, and all around,
    Beat the free foot on the ground,
    While the white man hunts his grave,
    You have won your vengeance, brave!

Marion Muir Richardson, *Border Memories* (Denver: published by
the author, 1903), pp. 17-18.

OLD MEN ON THE BLUE

By *Thomas Hornsby Ferril*

Our last remaining prospectors sit in the shade of an old mining
town storefront and watch our world go by. Colorado's outstanding
poet, Thomas Hornsby Ferril, so describes the old men of Breckenridge, Colorado.

I know a barn in Breckenridge on the Blue,
In summit County, Colorado, where
A Ford transmission rots upon the wall
Beside an ox-yoke. You can stand inside
The barn and peer like a pack-rat through the logs
And see how summertime looks outdoors, and see
A sleigh with hare-bells ringing under it,
And snowy yarrow drifting over the runners.

How high the mountains are behind the barn
Along toward evening nobody seems to know,
And nobody seems to know how blue they are,
Not even the old men sitting all day long
On a ledge in the shade in front of the general store;
But they watch the gasoline go up and down
In the big glass pump where the white-faced people stop
Who are crossing the Rocky Mountains.

They watch the white-faced people crawl away
Into the hackled fractures of the peaks,
Up where the Mississippi River ends
And the bodies of the frozen dragonflies
Begin to float to the Gulf of California.

The mountain ranges in the evening fill
The sockets of the old men's eyes with blue,
And some of their cheeks are lavender and lilac.
One long day after sunset sunlight poured
Out of the east, from an amber thunderhead,
To make their cheek-bones shine like yellow gold.

The old men do not speak while the pump is running,
But when you drive away you can hear their voices,
Like sounds you hear alone at night in a canyon
When pieces of blackness clatter on pieces of water,
And you think if you didn't have the car in low,
You could overhear what the mountains have never told you.

At night the old men sleep in houses that
Will always have geraniums in the windows.

Thomas Hornsby Ferril, *Westering* (New Haven: Yale University Press, 1934), pp. 60-61. Reprinted by special permission of the author and of the publisher.

II

COWBOYS AND CATTLE

A VETERAN COWBOY'S RUMINATIONS

By John M. Kuykendall

The cowboy, in the decades following the Civil War, developed a distinctive costume and a unique way of life. In the following lines an old cattleman recalls his companions of the earlier days.

Oft times I get to thinkin' of the changes times has wrought
Since upon the Western ranges long ago I cast my lot,
Of the days when yaller Injuns was a roaming everywhere
Keepin' us oneasy for the safety of our hair.
I was young and full o' ginger in them days of long ago,
Now my limbs are all rheumatic an' my head is teched with snow,
An' I often git comparin' of the cowboy of today
With the weather-tanned ol' riders, now respectable and gray.

Didn't have no dandy riders with their fancy-bosom shirts,
Didn't have no love-knot ribbons tied by gals upon our quirts,
Didn't pack no looking glasses in our saddle bags, to see
If the wind an' our complexion seemed inclined fur to agree
Didn't wear no chaparejos trimmed with fringes an' with beads
Fur to keep our tailor breeches from the bushes an' the weeds,
An' you bet you never saw us, it's as true as preachin', boss,
With a hundred dollar saddle on a twenty dollar hoss.

Wan't no shindigs at the ranches, as they have them now-a-days,
With a lot of purty cowgals fur to jine in the hoorays,
Whar the music of the fiddle started every heart to prance,
An' the gods of fun and frolic ruled the sperrit of the dance.
Then we lived in tents and dugouts, jest some blankets fur our beds,
Used our saddles then for pillows onto which to lay our heads,
An' our rifles an' our pistols right beside us we would lay,
So's to get 'em poco pronto if the Injuns made a play.

Does me good to get a thinkin' of them days of old lang syne,
An' about my ol' companions, now away up in the line;
Texas Jim, a holy terror, wild an' reckless, brave an' bold,
Now a high-toned legislator up in Denver, I am told.
Lazy Sam from Arizony, no account from head to toes,
Is a lawyer in Pueblo wearin' tailor-fashioned clothes,

53

An' ol' Ligh'nin' Jack McGinnis, allus spoilin' for a fight,
In the church at Kansas City is a bright and shining light.

Hungry Tom, a fiend for eatin', got quite rich I understand,
An' is now back thar in congress slingin' style to beat the band,
An' ol' Andy Duzenberry, I am quite surprised to hear,
Holds a guv'ment position with a fortune every year.
But the news that most surprised me, was that Swearin' Tommy Bell
Him that used to snear at heaven an' to crack his jokes at hell,
Toughest cuss on all the ranges with their tough outfits of boys,
Is a preachin' of the gospel, back in Southern Illinois.

I'm the only sole survivor of the cowboys of the past,
That has stuck to cowboy customs, an' I'll hold them to the last.
An' I often sit an' wonder if them good ol' boys and I
Will be apt to drift together to the home ranch up on high,
Often wonder if they'll know me, and I'll recognize ol' Shaw
That was with them punchin' cattle down along the Arkansaw.
An' if they'll be 'shamed to own me if I ain't so stylish dressed
Whar the wicked cease from troublin' an' the weary are at rest.

From *The Trail*, vol. II, no. 8 (Denver, January, 1910), p. 17.

CODE OF THE COW COUNTRY

By S. Omar Barker

Like the European knights of old, the cowboy created for himself
an idealistic, not entirely mythical, standard of conduct.

> It don't take sech a lot o' laws
> To keep the rangeland straight,
> Nor books to write 'em in, because
> They's only six or eight.

> The first one is the welcome sign
> Wrote deep in Western hearts:
> "My camp is yours an' yours is mine"
> In all cow country parts.

Treat with respect all womankind,
    Same as yuh would your sister.
Take care o' neighbor's strays yuh find,
    An' don't call cowboys "mister."

Shet pasture gates when passin' through;
    An' takin all in all,
Be jest as rough as pleases you,
    But never mean nor small.

Talk straight, shoot straight, an' never break
    Your word to man nor boss.
Plumb always kill a rattlesnake.
    Don't ride a sorebacked hoss.

It don't take law nor pedigree
    To live the best yuh can!
These few is all it takes to be
    A cowboy an' . . . a man!

S. Omar Barker, *Buckaroo Ballads* (Santa Fe: New Mexican Publication Corp., 1928), p. 123. Reprinted by special permission of the author.

OLD BUCK'S GHOST

By Frank Benton

One of the favorite tales of early cattle days related how an innocent British buyer was tricked into buying many times over a herd which was driven round and round a hill. The buyer has been named as one of the Frewen Brothers of the Powder River Cattle Company, in Wyoming; but Moreton Frewen, in his book, *Melton Mowbray*, denied that anything of the kind had happened to him when, in the summer of 1879, he bought the 76 brand from Tim Foley. But no amount of denial can exorcise a good legend.

Down in New Mexico, where the plains are brown and sere,
There is a ghostly story of a yellow spectral steer.
His spirit wanders always when the moon is shining bright,
One horn is lopping downwards, the other sticks upright.

On three legs he comes limping, as the fourth is sore and lame;
His left eye is quite sightless, but still this steer is game.
Many times he was bought and counted by a dude with a monocle in
   his eye;
The steer kept limping round a mountain to be counted by that guy.

When footsore, weary, gasping, he laid him down at last,
His good eye quit its winking; counting was a matter of the past;
But his spirit keeps a tramping 'round that mountain trail,
And that's the cause, says Packsaddle, that I have told this tale.

Frank Benton, *Cowboy Life on the Sidetrack* (Denver: The Western
Stories Syndicate, 1903), p. 55.

THE BRANDING IRON HERD

By Ralph Rigby

In 1884, Wyoming law defined "mavericks" and stated that all
foremen of roundup districts were to take up unbranded motherless
calves and sell them at auction on the range. Previously, these calves
became the property of the first man to slap his brand on them. Many
a man who came up the Texas trail as a cowboy created the basis for
a substantial fortune with nothing more than a "long rope and a
running iron."

Waal, yass, stranger, them's fine cows,
You bet your life. There was sev'ral rows.
'Bout the time that herd was started,
That was when I up and parted
From a Texas trail on my own behalf.
At that time I didn't own a calf,
And couldn't borrow in these environs,
But I got me a pair of branding irons,
That was my stock in trade, you bet;
Them hunky old irons — I've got 'em yet.
I've heerd as how tailors like their shears,
When they grow to big men in after years;
An' how a shoemaker toted his stool
When he got to know more'n any school;

56

An' how mechanics saved up their tools
When they got rich — They wasn't fools,
But they kept those things all through life
To show how they begun the strife,
An' how they riz from poor to rich,
To show they was tailor, shoemaker and sich.
Now that's the way with me, stranger.
I never thought, when I was a ranger,
I'd ever own a herd of cattle, —
But them pair of irons was half the battle.
A little range I call my own
Lay over a creek, and all alone
With my irons and me I watched
For mavericks. And every one I scotched
And put my brand onto his hide.
Yes, it was a little snide,
But wasn't them mavericks on my range?
And I tell you what, it's awful strange
If I couldn't brand calves that might belong
To me. At least my opinion was strong
That they did. Then it was on the plains
The custom; and when custom rains
Mavericks I ain't a going to kick.
But you bet I'll just put in my lick
And get all I can. That's what's what.
No, stranger; of late years I do not
Hunt for mavericks. I've got as many
As ten thousand head, as fine as any
Cattle you ever seen. And my name
Is good. My branding-iron fame
Is all wiped out. I lives up square
And I do everything on the fair.
I own fine houses, and hold big notes,
And reg'lar twice a year I totes
Them round for my two per cent
Per month. You see that's our rent
For cash in these parts. But never mind;
In the game of life I ain't a going blind,
But wait for threes, a full or a flush,
When I make the pot boil up like mush.

So you see that I have gotten along,
And nobody tells me I ever done wrong—
But I can't help thinkin', twixt you an' me,
And I know that on this point you'll agree,
That my start was small; only a few firin's,
And, you bet, the *boss pair* of branding irons.

From *The Cheyenne Daily Leader*, December 8, 1880.

HOT IR'N!

By S. Omar Barker

Since 2000 B. C., nothing has been found to take the place of "hot iron" branding as a permanent mark of cattle ownership.

The thumpin' sound o' hosses' hoofs, the clack o' runnin' cows,
    The song o' loopin' lassos on the swing,
The smell o' cedar fire, an' then to make yer pulses rouse,
    Yuh hear some cowboy beller forth an' sing:
            "Hot ir'n! Hot ir'n!
            Wup! Come on, snap it up!
            Hot ir'n!"

Yuh grab the red irons from the fire an' run to where he's downed
    A bawlin' calf an' holds him with his loop;
Yuh slap 'em on the hairy hide. The Ma cow bellers round
    An' makes a bluff at hookin' where yuh stoop.
            "Hot ir'n! Hot ir'n!
            Come, burn 'em 'Rafter Bell'!
            Hey! Bring 'em hot as hell!
            Hot ir'n!"

All day the ropers drag the calves from out the millin' herd,
    All day there's dust an' stink o' singein' hair!
The noise kinder makes yer ears buzz like a hummin' bird —
    Then raucous-squawkus hollers split the air:
            "Hot ir'n! Hot ir'n!
            Cain't hold this calf all day!
            Come on! Hey, what yuh say?
            Hot ir'n!"

It ain't the sweetest kind o' work — calf brandin' on the range —
  It's lots o' labor, dirt an' burnt hair smell,
But still I ain't a-hankerin' to see the old ways change,
  I kinder like to hear that raspin' yell:
        "Hot ir'n! Hot ir'n!
        This dogie here I've got
        Ull git up like as not!
        Hey, cowboy! Bring 'em HOT!
        HOT IR'N!"

S. Omar Barker, *Buckaroo Ballads* (Santa Fe: New Mexican Publishing Corp., 1928), pp. 15-16. Reprinted by special permission of the author.

INVASION SONG
A Ballad of the Wyoming "Rustler War"
Anonymous

In 1892, conflicts between the owners of large herds in Wyoming and bands of "rustlers," with whom were identified the small ranchers, came to a head in the so-called "Johnson County War. Contemporary newspaper reporting and the speedy writing of this war's history gave little chance for folk tradition to accumulate, but feeling ran high on both sides and today two versions of the struggle are still to be heard from the old-timers and their descendants. The following song, expressing the Johnson County point of view, was written down by W. A. Martin, a Wyoming cowboy and "Red" Angus deputy, who later lived near Fort Collins, Colorado. He noted that the ballad was sung at the conclusion of the trouble, in April, 1892, and was "composed (in part) by a drunken cowpuncher and set to music by one of Buffalo's 'soiled doves.' "

        Sad and dismal is the tale
          I now relate to you,
        'Tis all about the cattlemen,
          Them and their murderous crew.
        They started out on their man hunt,
          Precious blood to spill,
        With a gang of hired assassins
          To murder at their will.

God bless poor Nate and Nick
    Who gave their precious lives
To save the town of Buffalo,
    Its brave men and their wives.
If it hadn't been for Nate and Nick
    What would we have come to?
We would have all been murdered by
    Frank Canton and his crew.

Poor Nate Champion is no more,
    He lost his precious life,
He lies down in the valley
    Freed from all care and strife.
He tried to run the gantlet
    When they had burned his home
And Nick was lying lifeless,
    Lips wet with bloody foam.

The run was made; his doom was sealed,
    A fact you all know well.
They left his lifeless body there
    On the slope, above the dell.
No kindred near to care for him,
    To grasp his nerveless hand;
A braver man was never faced
    By Canton's bloody band.

The very next name upon the list
    Was that of brave Jack Flagg.
Frank Canton must have surely thought
    That he would "fill his bag."
Jack and his stepson came in view
    A-riding round the curve;
"Throw up your hands! By God they're off!"
    Frank Canton lost his nerve.

"Red Angus" next, the "Canny Scot,"
    Was marked for Canton's lead;
But Angus, warned by bold Jack Flagg,
    For aid and succor, sped.

The countryside now swarmed to life,
The settlers armed in haste;
Soon "Red" had hundreds at his back
Who Canton's minions faced.

To Crazy Woman's winding bank
The cowed invaders fled.
With K. C., blazing in their rear,
And Ray and Champion dead.
Here, held at bay the cravens halt
Till soldiers come to aid;
And now secure in jail they rest,
The debt of blood, unpaid.

From a manuscript provided by Mr. W. A. Martin.

EIGHTEEN-NINETY

By E. Richard Shipp

After the great influx of "woollies" into the cattle country in the nineties, the cattleman-sheepman feud ranged over the West and sometimes broke out into open warfare.

The old Cowman,
cross-legged, sat before the fire;
like oak-tanned leather
his smooth shaven face shone
in the flickering light.
His boys sat around and smoked.
He talked in quiet, level tone,
nor raised his voice,
what he said he meant,
what he did not say they knew he meant.

"Damn the Sheep!
They've ruined the range—
dug the grass out by the roots—
there's a bunch bedded down
over to the west

a mile or so from here,
not far from Red Canyon—
it drops straight down,
a hundred feet or more—
had some Cows go over there once,
we didn't even get their hides.
It's a bad place for stock
when they go on stampede.

"The hosses haint tired,
little exercise wont hurt 'em none.

"Think I'll roll in,
good-night, boys, and . . .
well . . . Damn the Sheep!"

E. Richard Shipp, *Rangeland Melodies* (Casper, Wyoming: Casper Stationery Co., 1923).

THE STAMPEDE

By Wallace D. Coburn

Cattle are skittish, and a herd can be stampeded by something considerably less than a lightning flash. The droning airs of cowboy songs were used by riders to soothe their charges, on peaceful nights.

Did you ever hear the story of how one stormy night,
A wild beef herd stampeded, down yonder to the right?
No? Well, you see that sloping hill, beyond the sagebrush flat,
East of the old round-up corral, where all the boys are at?
'Twas one night in November, and I was on first guard,
A storm was brewing in the west, the wind was blowing hard.
Of wild Montana steers we had about a thousand head,
Belonging to the "Circle C," and each one full of "Ned."
The season had been rainy, and the grass was thick and long,
So the herd had found good grazing in the hills the whole day long.
The clouds had piled up in the west, a strangely grotesque mass,
And the rain began to patter on the weeds and buffalo grass.

The lightning flared up in the clouds, and all was deathly still,
Except the melancholy howl of a coyote on the hill.
The vivid, shifting lightning kept bright the stormy scene,
And I could see the broken hills, with wash-outs in between.
And when Bill, who was standing first guard with me that night,
Came jogging past, he 'lowed that it certainly was a sight.
And then commenced to whistle, while I began to sing,
The lightning flared along the sky like demons on the wing.
But round and round rode Bill and me, with slickers buttoned tight,
And looking like dim specters in the constant changing light.
The thunder now began to peal and crash along the sky,
The cattle pawed and moved about, and the wind went whistling by.
Then, suddenly, without a sign, there came an awful crash,
And my eyes were almost blinded by a bright and burning flash
That filled the air an instant, then as suddenly went out,
While little sparks of lightning seemed floating all about.
And then the scene that followed defies my tongue to tell,
For those wild steers stampeded when the deadly lightning fell.
I don't know how it happened, but when my vision clears,
I find that I am riding in the midst of running steers.
And Oh! the thoughts that filled my brain as in that living tide
Of hoofs and horns and glowing eyes, I made that fearful ride.
On and on at deadly speed, I dared not slacken pace;
A stone wall could not stop us in that blood-curdling race.
And if a cowboy ever prayed with fervor in his prayer,
'Twas me among those madd'n'd beasts, for I prayed in despair.
My horse was jammed and thrown about as o'er the rocky ground
We sped like some vast torrent, with stubborn, sullen sound.
But when my horse was almost gone, and death stalked all about,
I heard above the awful roar a cowboy's ringing shout.
And looking backward in the gloom, I caught a fleeting glance
Of cowboys flitting to and fro, like spirits in a dance.
And then I felt my nerve come back, like some old, long-lost friend,
For I had given up all hope, and waited for the end.
At first I couldn't hardly tell just what they hoped to do,
But soon I saw they meant to cut that running herd in two.
For after chopping off a bunch, they lined up with a cheer,
To form a wedge of solid men and charge them from the rear.
Then on they came through tossing horns, with old Jack in the lead;
The cattle parted stubbornly, but didn't slacken speed.

On and on, with sturdy force, those brave lads struggled on,
But I doubted if they'd reach me before my horse was gone.
For, as I spurred his reeking flanks, and pulled his head up high,
He slowly sank beneath me, and I felt that I must die.
But up again he struggled, then down he went once more,
And I found myself a knockin' at old death's gloomy door.
And when I got my senses, the hoofs and horns were gone,
And Bill was kneeling at my side with streaming slicker on.
You see, my leg was broken and chest was badly crushed,
By half a dozen reckless steers, as over me they rushed.
But it's hard to kill a cowboy; they're pretty tough you know,
Else I'd been riding in the clouds with angels long ago.

Wallace D. Coburn, *Rhymes from a Round Up Camp* (n.p., 1899),
pp. 14-19.

THE STAMPEDE

By Earl Alonzo Brininstool

A later writer tells why the cowboy saw death in the sudden
thunderstorms of the plains.

A lowering night, with muggy sultry air;
 A thirsting, restless, sullen, bawling herd;
Low distant rumbling peals of thunder there;
 A sky with vivid lightning-flashes blurred.
The flickering campfire's dull and feeble glow;
 The ribald songs the grim night-herders sing;
The murmur of the river, faint and low;
 The night-bird over head, on tireless wing.

From rugged buttes, in snarling monotone,
 The muttering thunder speaks a warning grim;
The breeze which o'er the rolling height is blown,
 Sighs fitfully across the mesa's brim.
Now vagrant rain-drops kiss the dusty ground,
 As louder growls the thunder-notes on high;
The cattle low in terror at the sound,
 While anxious riders watch the threatening sky.

And now the storm bursts forth in fury wild,
    As jagged lightning-flashes leap and flare
Across the heavens, where inky clouds are piled,
    While crash on crash re-echoes through the air!
In mad affright the herd is under way!
    No hand their headlong rushes can restrain!
And blinding, glaring shafts of light display
    A sea of clashing horns across the plain!

Into the pitchy darkness of the night,
    With spur and quirt and shout and wild hello,
Lithe figures speed to check their frenzied flight,
    As on the panic-stricken thousands go!
            *   *   *   *
And now the Storm God's wrath is spent and gone;
    Hushed is his voice upon the mesa's crest;
The stars peep forth through scudding clouds, and dawn
    Finds wearied riders safe, the herd at rest.

E. A. Brininstool, *Trail Dust of a Maverick* (New York: Dodd, Mead
and Co., 1914), p. 13.

THE ROUND-UP

By Sarah Elizabeth Howard

Stampedes happened during roundups and pre-railroad "drives"
to market. This roundup picture uses a medium usually too formal
for the western poet: blank verse.

The lovely days of spring have clothed the plains
With fresh, sweet grass, and spread a welcome feast
Before the wandering herds. The cattlemen
Prepare to "round" their creatures "up," and learn
The loss or profit of the year. For weeks,
The country to be traversed, and the place
To meet each day with gathered herds, has been
Decided on, and advertised, that all
The owners with their men may gather where
Their cattle range, and do their share of work,—

And claim and brand their property. One man, —
A chosen Captain, — plans and orders all.
From every side they come with ponies fleet
Of foot, and trained to hold the struggling beasts
When rider's ropes have checked their utmost flight;
With cowboys skilled in throwing lariats,
And reading brands obscure, or tampered with;
With men to cook, and drive the wagons filled
With blankets and with food supplies to each
Day's camping place; with irons that shall brand
The owner's undisputed claim upon
The luckless calf. Prepared to live upon
The plains for weeks, — to sleep upon the ground
In blankets wrapped, these hardy plainsmen go
Far to the eastern limit of the range
Their cattle feed upon, and "round them up"
By sending riders on a circuit wide,
To gather every animal that shows
A brand belonging to the men for whom
They work. A camping place is chosen where
They wish to have the first day's round-up brought,
And there the cook is found, prepared to feed
The hungry men.
          The first red streak of dawn
Is signal for the start, and silently
The horsemen vanish on their tiring quest,
Each, with his ground to cover, pointed out.
The river flows upon the south, — some search
Its banks; another party follows up
A tributary stream, and others scour
The distant bluffs, and all the land between.
Well past the hour of noon, the cowboys with
The herd appear, and men detailed for their
Relief, ride out to guard the band, while they
Who gathered them, refresh the inner man.

Again, a mammoth stage, and actors skilled.
Around a smouldering fire a group of men
Are heating irons, each of which shall sear
Upon the owner's living property,

Its quaint device. The mounted cowboys, spurred,
With lariats in hand, dash in among
The herd, and singling out the animals
They want, — give chase. The race is short. The rope,
Well thrown, soon stops a creature's flight. Half dragged,
Half running, it is quickly taken where
The branders wait to do their work. Each man
Keeps tally of the calves he brands, and so
The census of the bovine family
That roams the plains, is taken. Animals
No longer wanted, are turned back upon
The range from whence they came; those held as beeves,
Or held to drive upon some other range,
Must be well guarded, day and night, and men
Take turns at that. With little change the work
Goes on from day to day. Each camping place
Is chosen for the chance it furnishes
Of water for the men and animals
And well for them if it may be a clear
And flowing stream. This hard exciting life
Is lived, until the prairies have been scoured
From Julesburg to the mountain towns, and well
Across Wyoming's line. Disbanded then,
The round-up waits another call.

Sarah Elizabeth Howard, *Pen Pictures of the Plains* (Denver: The Reed Publishing Co., 1902), pp. 99-103. Reprinted by special permission of the copyright holder, Mrs. Sadie Howard Johnson.

THE COWBOY'S FATE

By Wallace D. Coburn

The cowboy has never admitted that he is just another agricultural worker. In the wild days, he could look forward to a death more spectacular than that of Robert Frost's "Hired Man."

> One night on the fall beef round-up,
> In October of ninety-three,
> Jack and I stood guard together —
> This is what he said to me:

67

"Yes, Bill, times have changed a little,
　　Since we first learned how to ride;
Country's full of barbed wire fences,
　　And the range is not so wide.

"And, Bill, you are rich and happy,
　　Got a wife and lots of gold;
Been a man and stuck to business,
　　While I — well, I'm getting old.

"Yes, I've been in many places,
　　Sorter on the French qui vive;
Wouldn't get but just located,
　　When I'd up and have to leave.

"Have to pack my bed and vanish;
　　Pull out for the high divide;
Seek a new range, strike a cow ranch,
　　Settle down and try to ride.

"Get a good job on the round-up;
　　Make a stake and go to town,
There fill up on Injun whiskey,
　　Pull my gun and saunter 'roun'.

"Smoke the town and whip the sheriff,
　　Play 'em high, and shoot and shout,
Till the air was filled with music
　　And the people all hid out.

"Then I'd saddle up my private,
　　Fog the street lights on the run,
Till I struck the open prairie —
　　Then my painting job was done.

"That is why I'm here tonight, Bill;
　　Ridin' 'roun' this old beef herd,
Listening to the coyotes holler —
　　Echoes of the life I've blurred.

"And it seems like luck's against me,
　　Now that I am getting gray;
For you know the good, old sayin',
　　'Every dog will have his day.'

"I can't stand the hard knocks now, Bill,
　　That I used to think was fun;
And I'm like an old cow pony
　　That's forgotten how to run.

"Say, Bill; you may think I'm nervy,
　　Wouldn't ask if I was flush,
But a man can't stan' to winter
　　Like a dogie in the brush.

"And I thought I'd better ask, Bill,
　　If you'd let me have a show
Just to earn a winter's grub stake,
　　Even if it's shovelin' snow.

"For, you see, I ain't partic'lar
　　What I drive at now-a-days,
Just to earn an honest livin',
　　For it's steady work that pays.

"And a man can't make a fortune
　　Paintin' towns and gettin' drunk;
Tried it long enough to know, Bill;
　　Wish I'd all the coin I've sunk.

"Thanks; I knew 'twould be a cold day
　　When you wouldn't help me, Bill;
Didn't know jest where I'd winter,
　　And the weather's gettin' chill.

"These nights makes a feller wonder
　　Where his summer work has gone,
When the frost sticks to his whiskers,
　　And he needs a coonskin on.

"Hope we'll have a few more warm days,
    Till we get these cattle shipped,
For this wind cuts like a blizzard,
    Makes me feel like I'd been whipped.

"Two o'clock! Well, who'd 'a' thought it?
    Time has flew on angel's wings,
As I heard an eastern feller
    Tell a girl down at the Springs.

"So, I guess I'd better hurry
    And wake up the next relief —
Guess camp's over in that coolee,
    Just beyond the rocky reef.

"So long, Bill; I'll see you later!"
    And old Jack passed out of sight;
Gayly singing as he galloped
    To his death that stormy night.

For we found his lifeless body
    When the morning sun arose,
With the diamond frost still sparkling
    On his blood be-spattered clothes.

For, you see, his horse had fallen;
    Struck a hole, and Jack was caught,
With his head crushed on a boulder —
    Thus his tragic death was wrought.

Poor old Jack! Good hearted always,
    May his soul in peace abide,
Where good cow-boys ride in comfort,
    Far beyond the "Great Divide."

Wallace D. Coburn, *Rhymes from a Round Up Camp* (n.p., 1899),
pp. 76-83.

THE ROUNDUP COOK

By Robert V. Carr

In the land of hard-fried steaks, canned beans, and strong
Arbuckle's coffee, a cook who could boil water was a man of power.

There's good cooks and there's bad ones —
    No harm in bein' frank;
But, speakin' gener'ly, I'll say,
    A roundup cook's a crank.
There's something aggravatin' in
    The dealin' out of chuck,
That makes a man not care fer jokes,
    And feel down on his luck.

If you should think to doubt my word,
    Jes' go and sass a cook;
And then fer some deep hole to hide,
    Go take a sudden look.
While goin's good, you'd better go
    Before the hash-knife falls,
Before the boss of pots and pans
    Your frame in anger crawls.

But yet we sort of like the cook,
    And love to hear him say:
"Oh, you'd better come and git it,
    Or I'll throw it all away!"
And to his face — tho', privately,
    We cuss him now and then —
We brag upon his chuck and act
    Like perfect gentlemen.

Robert V. Carr, *Cowboy Lyrics* (Boston: Small, Maynard & Co.,
1912; privately printed, 1908), pp. 34-35.

WILD HORSE JERRY'S STORY

By Sarah Elizabeth Howard

Wild horses were often captured to fill out the "remuda" or "cavvy" for the working cowboy, who needed several changes of mount in a day. Some of the methods used are described in the following matter-of-fact verse.

All over this unsettled country, bands
Of wild and unowned horses roam, each band
Protected and controlled by one strong male.
This stallion will allow no rival near,
And weaker males are often found alone,
Upon the plains. Terrific fights sometimes
Ensue, when two aspire to leadership.
I followed once, for forty hours or more,
A band that was becoming very tired;
We chanced to pass upon the plains, one of
These lone and beaten males. He seemed at once
To know his hated rival's strength was gone,
And saw his chance to take the band from him.
They fought for mastery for more than half
A day, and reared, and struck, and bit, and fell
Upon their knees and wrestled terribly,
Until the lonely horse the leadership
Assumed, — made victor by his greater strength.
The man who captures these wild animals
Must test his patience and endurence well.
When I discover where they range, I make
My camp as near them as I can and still
Be near a good supply of water; then,
I place my men and extra horses there —
In camp — and ride out toward the wary band.
You know all horses cling to their old range,
And will not leave it unless driven off,
And then, when free, return. This instinct, — when
I only follow them enough to keep
Them moving, — causes them to circle some,
And makes it quite an easy thing for me
To have a new fresh horse from camp when mine

Is tired. Wild horses are intelligent,
And harder to surprise than antelope.
They see me when a mile away, and stand
And watch me for awhile, and when they learn
That I am nearing them, they run to some
Far hill and watch again. When they decide
That they are followed, then, the work begins.
They then will start and run for twenty miles,
Or more. I do not try to follow near
To them, but ride the way they went until
They notice me, and run again, and so
Allow them little time to eat, or sleep.
I always let them drink; they then become
More gentle and less active, too. I do
Not try to crowd them day and night, but try
To get them used to seeing me. A day
Or two, I work like this, and then ride near
To them, and in a measure can direct
Their course. The yearlings tire out first and want
To stop. One time, a leader tried to drive
Me back; as he came near to me I threw
Some rocks and hit him just behind the ear;
I felled him several times; at last, he kept
Away, but still showed fight. Three days and nights
I've followed these wild creatures, without sleep,
Excepting that I dozed a little as
I rode. The horses were so weary that
They could not travel fast, or far; I drove
Them very carefully into a strong
Corral, so made that it did not betray
It was a trap for them. If I had urged
Them then, they would have scattered, and my work
Would all have been in vain. The largest herd
I ever caught, was thirty. Men have stunned
And captured animals they coveted,
By "creasing" them; they wound with rifle ball
A certain cord upon the horse's neck,
Which causes him to fall unconscious; then,
They bind their prize, and hold him prisoner,
And while they cure the wound, they tame the horse.

It often happens that the bullet strikes
A vital point, an inch below the mark,
And then the noble creature murdered falls, —
A victim of man's cruelty and greed.

Sarah Elizabeth Howard, *Pen Pictures of the Plains* (Denver: The Reed Publishing Co., 1902), pp. 84-87. Reprinted by special permission of the copyright holder, Mrs. Sadie Howard Johnson.

COW-BOY FUN

By Wallace D. Coburn

Arrogant, young, caste-conscious, the cowboy in town was prone to the amusements of "single men in barracks."

"Yes, stranger, them was red-hot times,
    And things they wasn't slow
In this here little, one-hoss town
    Some twenty years ago.

"Cow punchers they was in their prime,
    And genteel in their ways,
And didn't ride the grub line, like
    You see 'em do now days.

"The ranges they was many,
    Where roamed the long-horned steer,
The wild horse and the buffalo;
    Likewise the elk and deer.

" 'Nd sheep — that robber of the range —
    Why, on these western hills,
If anyone had seen a sheep,
    'Twould have been a case of chills.

"Water it was plenty,
    And the lakes was overflowed;
The grass it waved like billows,
    When the western breezes blowed.

74

"The cow-boy, he wore notches on
    His ivory-handled gun,
To show the number of scraps
    That he had fought and won.

"There was Cussin' Sam, the captain,
    And Oklahoma Dick,
And City Jim, the same as had
    The fight on Beaver crick.

"Bill Riley he was in his prime,
    With Parson Sim, his chum;
And Tin-Horn Pete was twistin' bronks,
    And wasn't on the bum.

"Buck Berry he was then alive,
    And used to come to town
To circulate his money and
    To throw good licker down.

"And Slippery Jake, the gambler,
    A onery galoot,
Was dealin' faro 'cross the way,
    With skinnin' games to boot.

"Sich as loaded dice and montey,
    With marked cards, on the sly;
But one day he played solitaire
    Between the earth and sky.

"Old Dirty Dave, the round-up cook,
    He, too, was workin' then;
With Club-foot, Yank 'nd Greaser Bill,
    And old Panhandle Ben.

"While Cotton-Eye, the night hawk,
    Was then a top cow hand,
As reckless as they make 'em,
    And, you bet, he had the sand.

"The women folks, them days, was brave,
  And never seemed to care
To flirt and enter politics,
  Or rip around and tear.

"But come and have another drink,
  My throat is gettin' dry,
A-talkin' of them good, old times —
  Them happy days gone by.

"Gi' me some red-eye — that's the stuff —
  Jar loose an' let her run;
There's nothing like old forty-rod
  To open up the fun.

"Now, boys, let's have a stag dance,
  And celebrate, you know;
The kag is full of whiskey,
  And our pockets full of dough.

"Come, stranger, don't be bashful,
  This party ain't select;
Though you're a simple tenderfoot,
  The boys they won't object.

"Say, boys, let's find a shepherd,
  A herder, that's the cheese,
Like that old whiskey soaker
  With his dog between his knees.

"Come, Shep — you, over yonder,
  A talkin' to your dog;
This ain't no lunatic asylum;
  Come, let's have a clog.

"Oh! you don't know how it's done, hey?
  You're modest, that is all;
Come, boys, let's start the music;
  Now, herder, balance all.

"Start, now; you're up against it;
　　Close up your blattin' face;
That's good; now slide out for the hills,
　　Your dog has quit the chase.

"Go! Pull your freight and vanish!
　　Get out and split the breeze,
Shake off the wool that's in your clothes —
　　A little faster, please.

"Now, gentlemen, the air is cleared
　　Of that flea-bitten bum,
Put up your guns and wet your throats
　　With Casey's fightin' rum.

"Here's to the happy days of old,
　　When wages they was high;
Come, drink, you won't get licker
　　In the sweet bye and bye."

Wallace D. Coburn, *Rhymes from a Round Up Camp* (n.p., 1899),
pp. 24-32.

WHEN DUTCHY PLAYS THE MOUTH HARP
By Robert V. Carr

"Stag dances," at which individuals cut capers, were amusements
of the frontiersman and the womanless cowboy.

When Dutchy plays th' mouth harp,
　　All th' fellers gather 'round,
An' help on with th' music,
　　By a-stompin' on th' ground;
An' th' cook he cuts a shuffle,
　　An' the night hawk pats his hand,
When Dutchy plays th' mouth harp,
　　In a way to beat th' band.

When Dutchy plays th' mouth harp,
  An' we've cached our chuck away,
An' a-feelin' mighty foxy
  An' a feelin' mighty gay,
There's nothin' we like better
  Than to lend a pattin' hand,
When Dutchy plays th' mouth harp,
  In a way to beat th' band.

When Dutchy plays th' mouth harp —
  Plays a cake walk mighty fine —
'Tis then us ole cowpunchers
  Come a-steppin' down th' line;
Around th' fire shuffilin'
  An' a-pattin' of th' hand,
When Dutchy plays th' mouth harp,
  In a way to beat th' band.

Robert V. Carr, *Black Hills Ballads* (Denver: The Reed Publishing Co., 1902), p. 42.

BILL HALLER'S DANCE

By Robert V. Carr

Square dances suited best the cowboy's taste for individual and free movement.

They're tunin' up the orchestray down at old Bill Haller's;
He's the feller that they claim jes' beats all the callers
In the country 'round fer miles—old bow-legged feller;
Say, you ought to hear that cuss jes' git up and beller:

  Balance all and do-see-do,
  Rope her, tie her, let her go;
  Mill her 'round and kiss her there,
  Prom'nade all, you know where.

Choose your partners! H-m-m-m! well, yes, grab the next one after,
'T won't harm nothin' if you do shake the roof with laughter;

78

Fer it's joy-time, — Whoop-hi-ree! Come around a-prancin' —
'Cause there's nothin' like the time down at Haller's dancin'.

> She's your true love, you kin bet,
> There's no dead ones in that set!
> Lope her 'round and squeeze her there,
> Prom'nade all, you know where.

Hear them fiddles! Hain't they great! Suff'rin' Land o' **Lawdy!**
On the head set, show your style, come a-steppin' gawdy.
Come a-raggin' down the line, — Whoop-a-lorum! let her,
Seems to me there's nothin' that makes a man feel better.

> Mornin' is a mile away,
> Never 'spect to hit the hay;
> She's a-waitin' — wake up there!
> Prom'nade all, you know where.

Hear old Haller, hear him now, all above the funnin',
Jes' a-laughin', callin', too; keeps the thing a-runnin'.
Round me up and turn me loose! Let me go a-prancin';
All I want is jes' to yell down at Haller's dancin'.

> If you love her tell her so,
> Rope her, brand her, let her go;
> Round her up and hold her there,
> Prom'nade all, you know where.

Robert V. Carr, *Cowboy Lyrics* (Boston: Small, Maynard and Co.,
1912), pp. 7-9.

AT A COWBOY DANCE

By James Barton Adams

Amorous men with spurs on — the joy was unconfined.

Git yo' little sage hens ready,
    Trot 'em out upon the floor —
Line 'em up there, you cusses! Steady!
    Lively now! One couple more.
Shorty, shed that ol' sombrero;
    Bronco, douse that cigarette!
Stop yer cussin', Cassimero,
    'Fore the ladies. Now, all set!

Salute yer ladies all together!
    Ladies opposite the same;
Hit the lumber with yer leather!
    Balance all and swing yer dame!
Bunch the heifers in the middle!
    Circle stags, and doe-se-doe —
Pay attention to the fiddle;
    Swing her round an' off you go!

First four forward! Back to places!
    Second foller! Shuffle back!
Now you've got it down to cases!
    Swing 'em till their trotters crack!
Gents all right a heel an' toein'!
    Swing 'em: kiss 'em if you kin!
On to next an' keep a-goin'
    Till yo' hit yer pards agin!

Gents to center; ladies round 'em!
    Form a basket; balance all!
Whirl yo' gals to where yo' found 'em;
    Promenade around the hall!
Balance to yo' pards and trot 'em
    Round the circle double quick!
Grab and kiss 'em while you've got 'em!
    Hold 'em to it if they kick!

Ladies, left hand to yer sonnies!
    Aleman! Grand right and left!
Balance all an' swing yo' honies —
    Pick 'em up an' feel their heft!
Promenade like skeery cattle!
    Balance all, an' swing yer sweets!
Shake yer spurs and make 'em rattle!
    Keno! Promenade to seats.

James Barton Adams, *Breezy Western Verse* (Denver: The Post Printing and Publishing Co., 1889), pp. 103-104.

THE COWBOY'S BALL

By Henry Herbert Knibbs

The cowboy sometimes discovered that there is more to a dance than acrobatics.

Yip! Yip! Yip! Yip! tunin' up the fiddle;
    You an' take yo'r pardner there, standin' by the wall!
Say "How!" make a bow, and sashay down the middle;
    Shake yo'r leg lively at the Cowboys' Ball.

Big feet, little feet, all the feet a-clickin';
    Everybody happy and the goose a-hangin' high;
Lope, trot, hit the spot, like a colt a-kickin';
    Keep a stompin' leather while you got one eye.

Yah! Hoo! Larry! would you watch his wings a-floppin',
    Jumpin' like a chicken that is lookin' for its head;
Hi! Yip! Never slip, and never think of stoppin',
    Just keep yo'r feet a-movin' till we all drop dead!

High heels, low heels, moccasins and slippers;
    Real ole rally 'round the dipper and the keg!
Uncle Ed's gettin' red — had too many dippers;
    Better get him hobbled or he'll break his leg!

Yip! Yip! Yip! tunin' up the fiddle;
  Pass him up another for his arm is gettin' slow.
Bow down! right in town — and sashay down the middle;
  Got to keep a-movin' for to see the show!

Yes, mam! Warm, mam? Want to rest a minute?
  Like to get a breath of air lookin' at the stars?
All right! Fine night. — Dance? There's nothin' in it!
  That's my pony there, peekin' through the bars.

Bronc, mam? No, mam! Gentle as a kitten!
  Here, boy! Shake a hand! Now, mam, you can see;
Night's cool. What a fool to dance, instead of sittin'
  Like a gent and lady, same as you and me.

Yip! Yip! Yip! tunin' up the fiddle;
  Well, them as likes the exercise sure can have it all!
Right wing, lady swing, and sashay down the middle . . .
  But this beats dancin' at the Cowboys' Ball.

Henry Herbert Knibbs, *Riders of the Stars* (Boston: Houghton Mifflin Co., 1916), pp. 79-80.

ROMANCE OF THE RANGE

By Robert V. Carr

Here is the pattern of legendary range romance: the cowboy and the schoolmarm, as set by Owen Wister in *The Virginian*, 1902, the same year that this poem was published.

She's bin out here a-teachin' fer this winter now a-past,
An' I hear that she's a-tellin' that this winter is her last —
That she's goin' to quit the schoolroom an' goin' home to stay —
An' somehow I'm jes' hatin' fer to see her go away.

For us fellers think that schoolmarm is an angel; yes we do,
A little blue-eyed angel, yet a woman thro' an' thro';
An' she treats us all so kindly, jes' th' same most ev'ry day,
An' somehow I'm jes' hatin' fer to see her go away.

She hain't never give me reasons fer to think I'd have a show
To win her, but I'm honest when I say I like her so,
That I dread her time fer goin', count ev'ry passin' day,
'Cause I'm hatin', jes' a hatin', fer to see her go away.

Well, her term is 'bout completed an', say, I don't think I
Have got th' nerve to greet her an' to say a last good-by;
Seems so tough! Oh, well, I'm feelin' — call it heartsick, if you may —
An' I'm hatin', jes' a-hatin', fer to see her go away.

Later.

Oh, say, I'm 'bout as happy as a feller wants to be;
Went to see her, an', by hookie, she jes' upped an' cried — you see
Right there I had to say it, what so long I've feered to say,
An' now we've went an' fixed it so she'll never go away.

Robert V. Carr, *Black Hills Ballads* (Denver: The Reed Publishing Co., 1902), pp. 63-64.

COWBOY'S SALVATION SONG
By Robert V. Carr

Like the pastoral Hebrews, our western cattle herders used the imagery of their trade for religious expression. This poem condenses most of that imagery, but is remarkable for not mentioning the "Great Divide."

Oh, it's move along, you dogies, don't be driftin' by th' way,
For there's goin' to be a round-up an' a cuttin' - out they say,
Of all th' devil's dogies an' a movin' at sunrise,
An' you'd better be preparin' fer a long drive to th' skies.

Oh, it's move along, you dogies, don't be driftin' by the way,
Fer th' boss of all th' rus'lers is a-comin' 'round to-day.
So you'd better be a-movin', throw your dust right in his eyes,
An' hit th' trail a-flyin' fer th' home-ranch in th' skies.

So it's move along, you dogies, fer th' devil has in hand
A bunch of red-hot irons an' he's surely goin' to brand

All his dogies, an' some others, an' mighty suddin, too,
So you'd better be a-movin' so he won't be brandin' you.

So it's move along, you dogies, tho' you have th' mange o' sin,
There's a range you're sure to shake it when you come a-trailin' in,
Where th' grass is allers growin' an' th' water's allers pure,
So it's move along, you dogies, 'fore th' devil brands you sure.

Robert V. Carr, *Cowboy Lyrics* (Boston: Small, Maynard and Co.,
Co., 1902), p. 27.

THE RANGE RIDER'S SOLILOQUY
By *Earl Alonzo Brininstool*

The cowhand's religious imagery has become a convention of
popular songs and popular poetry.

Sometimes when on night-herd I'm ridin', and the stars are a-gleam in
  the sky,
Like millions of wee, little candles that twinkle and sparkle on high,
I wonder, if up there among 'em, are streets that are shinin' with gold,
And if it's as purty a country as all the sky-pilots hev told?

I wonder if there are wide ranges, and rivers and streams that's as clear,
And plains that's as blossomed with beauty as them that I ride over
  here?
I wonder if summertime breezes up there are like zephyrs that blow
And croon in a cadence of sweetness and harmony down here below?

I wonder if there, Over Yonder, it's true that they's never no night,
But all of the hours are sunny and balmy and pleasant and bright?
I wonder if birds are a-singin' as sweetly through all the long day
As them that I hear on the mesa as I go a-lopin' away?

And sometimes I wonder and wonder if over that lone Great Divide
I'll meet with the boys who have journeyed across to the dim Farther
  Side?
If out on them great starry ranges some day in the future, I, too,
Shall ride on a heavenly bronco when earth's final round-up is
  through?

They tell us no storms nor no blizzards blow over that bloom-spangled
   range;
That always and ever it's summer — a land where there's never a
   change;
And nights when I lie in my blankets, and the star-world casts o'er
   me a spell,
I seem to look through on the glories that lie in that great Home
   Corral.

E. A. Brininstool, *Trail Dust of a Maverick* (New York: Dodd, Mead
and Co., 1914), pp. 22-23.

THE OLD COWBOY'S LAMENT

By Robert V. Carr

Historians mark the "beginning of the end" of the western
frontier, with the enclosing of the ranges, in 1890.

The range's filled up with farmers and there's fences ev'rywhere,
   A painted house 'most ev'ry quarter mile;
They're raisin' blooded cattle and plantin' sorted seed,
   And puttin' on a painful lot o' style.

There hain't no grass to speak of and the water holes are gone,
   The wire of the farmer holds 'em tight;
There's little use to law 'em and little use to kick,
   And mighty sight less use there is to fight.

There's them coughin' separaters and their dirty, dusty crews,
   And wagons runnin' over with the grain;
With smoke a-driftin' upward and writin' on the air,
   A story that to me is mighty plain.

The wolves have left the country and the long-horns are no more,
   And all the game worth shootin' at is gone;
And it's time fer me to foller, 'cause I'm only in the way,
   And I've got to be a movin' — movin' on.

Robert V. Carr, *Cowboy Lyrics,* (Boston: Small, Maynard and Co.,
1912), pp. 71-72.

RODEO DAYS

By S. Omar Barker

The cowboy's tournament of professional skills has become a major sport, a standardized western spectacle, and big business.

Ropin' of yearlin's and tyin' 'em down,
Wrastlin' of steers so the folks from town
Once in their lives gits a chance fer to see
Wild "hook 'em cowboys" like you and like me.

Straddlin' of broncos jest out of the chutes,
Forkin' 'em bareback like Injun Piutes,
Rakin' the shoulders of bellerin' steers,
Hearin' the audience whoopin' their cheers.

Milkin' wild cows and a-ridin' wild mules,
Wearin' silk shirts and a'yellin' like fools,
Cowboys is in from the ranches in dozens
Whoopin' 'em up fer their city cousins.

Dancin' all night and a-raisin' the deuce,
Millin' the streets like a loco cayuse —
Seems kinder funny fer us quiet boys
To raise so much rumpus and rouse so much noise!

Buckin' the contests we play at a battle
Learned on the ranges a-workin' with cattle.
What we put on ain't no circusy show,
It's workaday stuff, this here wild rodeo!

Makin' a game of rough skill and of muscles,
Lettin' America witness our tussels
Born of frontierin' and dear to the hearts
Of every old waddy in these western parts.

Rodeo time is fer rompin' and rarin'
Ridin' and ropin' and doin' yer darin' —

They say the cowboy is doomed fer to go —
Hi-yip! We've still got the ol' rodeo!

S. Omar Barker, *Buckaroo Ballads* (Santa Fe: New Mexican Publishing Co., 1928), p. 38. Reprinted by special permission of the author.

WESTERN FORMULA

Anonymous

Cowboy stories in pulp magazines, in the movies, on the radio, and as a mainstay of television, torment moderns as much as the knightly romances tormented Don Quixote.

A caow-hand with a gun or two,
We'd better call him Tex or Slim;
A ranch gal by the name of Sue
Who's lost the love she held for him,
She's fallen for a city slicker;
The slicker wears a waxed moustache,
He draws his gun a trifle quicker —
We'll call the ranch the old X-Dash.

The cook, a Chink, is in the plot;
A caow-hand strums on his guitar;
A coyote howls with all he's got;
A shot is heard from yonder bar;
A band of Injuns yells and whoops
And ford a crick called Powder River;
They battle with our gallant troops;
The ranchman's wife and children shiver.

But Slim, the hero, saves the day
And proves the city dude a killer;
So Sue and Slim now ride away —
And there's your sure-fire Western Thriller.

From *Author and Journalist*, Denver, February, 1941, p. 9. Reprinted by special permission of Alan Swallow, editor.

III

INDIANS, SCOUTS AND SOLDIERS

THE GATHERING ON THE PLAINS

By William T. Butler

The great struggle for the buffalo plains of the West between the Indians and the oncoming white men was largely decided by the building of transcontinental railroads soon after the Civil War. A contemporary magazine versifier aptly described the historical situation in the following composition and showed, at the same time, considerable sympathy for the still dangerous "red savages," usually hated by frontiersmen.

From the far-off Rocky Mountains, where they meet the eastern hills,
From the cradles where great rivers are but puny infant rills,
From the hunting-grounds and war-paths of the red men unsubdued,
Comes a savage yell of vengeance, comes a cry of blood for blood.

The Fort Phil Kearney garrison recked not that they were few;
Trained soldiers of the Union, they were veteran "boys in blue."
They'd all the white man's pride and trust in white men's blood and
    brains;
They despised the mountain Indians and the Indians of the plains.

The braves of mountain, plain, and hill were many, and they knew,
As well as General Grant himself, what "men enough" can do.
They trapped the fourscore "boys in blue" within a pathless glen;
With thousands they surrounded them, and fourscore scalps were ta'en.

No longer from the East alone doth emigration pour,
A tide is flowing mountainward from the Pacific's shore.
New York and San Francisco meet beneath Montana's pines,
And work together in the depths of Colorado's mines.

Like shipwrecked sailors cast upon a sea-surrounded shoal,
O'er which the waves remorselessly at high-tide time will roll;
The Indians see a swelling flood of white men brave and keen,
Advancing from the east and west, and hemming them between.

Already has this swelling flood surged ominously near
The pastures of the buffalo, the coverts of the deer;
The prairie dog, the foot-hill wolf, the savage grizzly bear,
Have scented the advancing tide that taints their native air.

The red man sees the changes vast a few short years have wrought,
And wonder, fear, and hate unite to cloud his troubled thought.
He sees the white man desecrate the graves of chief and sage,
And lord it o'er his hunting-grounds, his children's heritage.

He sees him everywhere intrude, and from where'er his feet
Leave footprints on the plain or hill, the red man must retreat.
He sees the cabin's smoke arise above the whispering pines,
He sees the tents, like sentinels, stand guard around the mines.

And where the squatter's hut is raised, by lake, or stream, or wood,
The red man's rights are but as sand before Missouri's flood.
And where the miner's tent is pitched, and white men work for hire,
The red man's wigwam is but grass before the prairie fire.

The white man's iron pathways strange, the trails and war-paths break,
His iron horse's shrieking neigh the foot-hill echoes wake.
From east to west, from west to east, his guarded wagon trains
Are toiling through the passes steep and stretching o'er the plains.

He's building bridges o'er the streams, and mills by all the falls,
His wondrous endless whispering wire the Indian brave appalls.
E'en nature's boldest barriers he conqueringly assails,
He is cutting down the mountains, he is filling up the vales.

On every side the potent signs of domination stand;
The red man's future is ignored, his name's writ in the sand.
Where shall he turn? where rear his lodge? where hunt, when far
    and near
The game is disappearing? Must the red man disappear?

No! No! from plain and mountain-side, from valley, hill, and glen,
Ascends the war-whoop's challenge fierce from thirty thousand men.
Tribes heretofore belligerent now own fraternal ties,
No longer are they enemies, but brothers and allies.

And e'en as trusting brothers band, when strangers dare intrude
To plunder their inheritance and ostracize their blood —
As soldiers rally 'neath their flag that ne'er hath known a stain —
So band and rally all the braves of mountain, hill, and plain.

From the Gila's sunny valleys, where the ice-breath of the north
Never ventures to blow rudely, comes the fierce Apache forth.
He is armed with Colt's revolvers (Indian traders trade so free!),
And he's mounted as a horse-thief from Durango ought to be.

From the plains of Western Texas, where the buffalo still feed,
Comes the warrior Comanche on his Coahuila steed.
But yesterday he dared the fight with quiver, lance, and bow; —
With rifle and revolver he now rides to meet the foe.

The Poncas, Moquis, Mandans, Sioux, Cheyennes, Arapahoes;
The Pawnees and the Pah-Utahs, the Blackfeet and the Crows,
And many other warlike tribes are mustering in their might,
To hold their ancient hunting-grounds and guard the red man's right.

The western breeze comes shuddering, and whispers from the lakes,
That when the snow has left the plains, and when the grass awakes,
The savage war-whoop will be heard, vengeance will seek her food,
And forts and frontier settlements will all be scenes of blood.

From *Harper's New Monthly Magazine,* Vol. XXV (June, 1867), pp.
120-121.

SONG OF THE NAVAJO

By Albert Pike

Boston-reared Albert Pike was probably the first Anglo-Saxon
poet to attempt to record the details and the "feel" of life in the
Rockies and the Southwest. He cast his impressions, gained by a
brief residence in Santa Fe and Taos, into an imitation of Byron's
then-popular *Hebrew Melodies.*

Who rideth so fast as a fleet Navajo?
Whose arm is so strong with the lance and the bow?
His arrow in battle as lightning is swift;
His march is the course of the mountainous drift.

The Eutaw can ride down the deer of the hills,
With his shield ornamented with bald-eagle quills;

Our houses are full of the skins he has drest;
We have slaves of his women the brightest and best.

Go, talk of the strength of a valiant Paiut,
He will hide in the trees when our arrows we shoot;
And who knows the wild Coyotera to tame,
But the bold Navajo, with his arrow of flame?

The Moqui may boast from his town of the Rock;
Can it stand when the earthquake shall come with its shock?
The Suri may laugh in his desert so dry;
He will wail to his God when our foray is nigh.

Oh, who is so brave as a mountain Apache?
He can come to our homes when the doors we unlatch,
And plunder our women when we are away;
When met he our braves in their battle array?

Whose mouth is so big as a Spaniard's at home?
But if *we* rush along like the cataract foam,
And sweep off his cattle and herds from his stalls,
Oh then to the saints who so loudly can call?

Up, then, and away! Let the quiver be full!
And as soon as the stars make the mountain air cool,
The fire of the harvest shall make heaven pale,
And the priesthood shall curse, and the coward shall wail.

And there will be counting of beads then to do —
And the Pueblos shall mount and prepare to pursue;
But when could their steeds, so mule-footed and slow,
Compare with the birds of the free Navajo?

Albert Pike, *Prose Sketches and Poems, Written in the Western Country* (Boston: Light and Horton, 1834), pp. 131-132.

THE LEGEND OF GRAND LAKE

By Judge Joseph L. Westcott

This is a white man's version of a Ute legend, told by an Indian to Judge Westcott, the reputed first white settler, in 1867, on the shores of Grand Lake, Colorado. Another version of the poem, printed by Mary Lyons Cairns in *Grand Lake: The Pioneers* (Denver: World Press, 1946), details in six additional pages the revenge taken by the main Ute band upon the Arapahoes. She notes that it was first published in the *Grand Lake Prospector* in "the early eighties." Other stories have it that the white mists which sometimes hover over Grand Lake are the spirits of the long-lost Indian women and children.

"White man, pause and gaze around, for we tread on haunted ground."
So said a chief to me one day, as along the shore we wound our way.
"Tell me, chieftain," then I said, "About this fight so fierce and red,
For I have often heard before, of this desperate fight in days of yore."
Silent and still the chieftain stood. He gazed the while at Lake
and wood.
Then silence deep was broke. In murmered tones these words he
spoke:

"On the same grounds where we now stand, once was encamped a
happy band,
One hundred warriors as true and brave as ever slept in warrior's
grave;
Squaws and papooses, eight score or more, were with us here on the
sandy shore.
Thirty-four years have sped away since the close of that fatal day.
The noble leader of our band, the bold chief Cheikiwow;
To man no better heart was given, no better soul ever reached
heaven.
Many a bright day we'd been camped there, with no thought of
trouble or fear.
But the dread hour was at hand, the annihilation of our band.
When a dark and dismal night set in, there would rise a horrid din.
Ghosts and goblins gathered round and made night hideous with
their sound.

Often some wild unearthly wail, borne on the zephyrs of the gale,
Would wake us from our troubled rest and send a cold chill through
    our breast.
And o'er the lake, so cold and deep, unearthly forms would upward
    leap,
Uttering a cry of woe and pain and dive into the deep again.
Such horrid sights our souls oppressed, such dismal sound disturbed
    our rest.
Thus the dark hours wore away until the dawn of that fatal day,
There never dawned a morn more bright that was followed by such
    a dismal night.
Alas, how many of our band would next day be in spirit land.

"I strolled to meet the evening breeze that broke so freshly through
    the trees,
And viewed the country far and nigh — the mount, the vale, the
    trees, the sky.
But, Hark! What means that low dull sound, slowly rolling along
    the ground?
Is it thunder that I hear, or is it a band of elk or deer?
And, Hark! That rumbling sound again is slowly rolling o'er the
    plain —
And now, far away to the west, I see the storm cloud's dismal crest.
And as I gazed the storm clouds grew until the scene was hid from
    view,
The wild coyote cried and screamed, and on every side the lightning
    gleamed.

"Cheikiwow had given command that every warrior of the band
Should arm and be prepared to fight, for danger hovered round that
    night.
The whole heavens were overcast and nearer came the howling blast.
The bright forked lightning wildly flashed, and deeptoned thunder
    loudly crashed.
Now from afar came the gray wolf's howl, and the dismal hoot of
    the big horned owl;
The panther's scream and the lion's roar echoed round from shore
    to shore.
The whole wild heavens overhead was covered over with bloody red.

High in midair engaged in strife, fiercely contending, life against life,
The phantom warriors fought and fell, and plainly was heard each
    ghastly yell.
Cheikiwow stood still, without a sound, and gazed upon the fury
    all around;
Then, in sorrowing tones, he said, in a breath: 'Such signs portend
    carnage and death —
The passing away from earthly strife to the happy hunting grounds
    of life.
Among the traditions of our band, there was never known through
    all the land,
Such horrid scenes and ghastly sights as we have seen on the last
    three nights.'

"Dark and dismal the night sat in, and on every side arose a din.
The ghost's wild shriek and the goblin's wail was borne on the crest
    of the coming gale.
Those dark red clouds had changed their hue, and dark as death
    appeared to view.
Terrified by the terrible din the scouts and the guards had all come
    in;
But, hark! Another cry we hear, that fills our hearts with boding
    fear —
That well-known cry so sharp and shrill is the clear-cut note of the
    whippoorwill.
Scarce had its echo died away when there appeared in fierce array,
And from every rock and shrub arose the fierce Cheyennes and
    Arapahoes;
Then from each painted warrior's throat across a defiant wild war
    note.
And at the same time a drenching rain burst o'er lake and rock and
    plain.
The arrowy tempest fell around and struck trees and rocks and
    ground,
But others, more true, with deadly aim, stretched warriors bleeding
    on the plain,
And on every side all around about came the gray wolf's howl and
    the foeman's shout.
Wilder grew the dreadful fight, still more dismal grew the night.
Half a score of friends were slain, and twenty foes lay on the plain.

The fearful charge our foeman made, a wall of death their progress
stayed.

The ground was strewn with mangled dead, and back again they
quickly sped,

Like lightning darting from on high, like meteors flashing through
the sky;

With bristling spear and wild war yell, full in their midst we fiercely
fell.

Where'er our noble chieftain turned, the battle there more fiercely
burned;

When he raised his battle-ax on high, a painted foe was sure to die.

Though fierce they fought and fast they fell, there still arose the
wild war yell;

Both friends and foes were falling fast, as thick as snow in winter
blast.

"We sped back to our post again, pursued by a most deadly rain;

The arrowy stream sped fiercely by, and many brave souls lay down
to die;

Full forty Utes were lying dead and a four score foeman's lives had
fled.

On logs and rafts, tied near at hand, our squaws and papooses had
left land,

And were borne away from the merciless shore, never to live on this
earth more.

"The foeman's chief, Red Wolf by name, a leader with a giant frame,

Whose war-like form bore many a scar, received in many a bloody
war,

It was his boast that no single foe could cope with him with spear
or bow;

No human foe before him stood but what he shed his foeman's
blood.

That blood-stained chief, that fearful night met Cheikiwow in single
fight.

Each chieftain stood transfixed, amazed; each at the other keenly
gazed.

Then high aloft each held his hand, and the battle ceased at their
command,

Each warrior's spear was leveled low, lowered at once was each
drawn bow.

Each chieftain clasped the other's hand before the eyes of their command.

And then they spoke to each other in accents low, but what they said we'll never know.

Then each drew forth his long stiff bow, and gave to the string a barbed arrow;

The barbed shaft sped through the sky, but from their shields dropped harmless by,

Again and again they shot, but still each time the missiles caught.

The useless bow was cast aside, the fatal spear its place supplied.

The deadly spears flew thick and fast like hailstones in the Autumn blast.

Blood flowed from many a gaping wound, and trickled slowly to the ground.

The cold sweat stood on Red Wolf's brow, he met his match in Cheikiwow.

At last from Cheikiwow came a dexterous stroke, and Red Wolf's spear was shattered and broke.

But Cheikiwow, you must all know, would never strike an unarmed foe;

He threw his spear against a rock, and it was shattered by the shock.

Now each chieftain drew his knife, continuing the deadly strife.

The last fierce thrust then Red Wolf made, but Cheikiwow the death blow stayed.

His knife flashed like a flaming dart and pierced Red Wolf to the heart.

Our foeman's chief tottered and fell, uttering at last one dying yell.

"A moment's silence reigned around, and then was broke by murmuring sound;

That murmur increased to a wail, and soon was followed by a howling gale.

Black Bear, the second in command, is now the leader of the band.

'Exterminate this hostile tribe, leave not a single foe alive,'

He cries in accents fierce and loud to his wild and murderous crowd.

'Cast every spear — spring every bow against Cheikiwow and lay him low,

For e'er the dawn of another day, his soul from earth must pass away.'

Against that single manly form showered that fearful deadly storm.

We strove in vain our chief to save, to spare him from a bloody grave;
But Cheikiwow felt that death was nigh, that e'er the morning he
must die.
He raised his battleaxe on high and loudly rang his battle cry.
And upon our foeman's ranks he fell, shouting the while his wild
war yell.
His battleaxe fell crushing down, cleaving a warrior through the
crown;
To right and left, with giant force, he bore destruction in his course.
His gallant form was failing fast, those sinewy limbs must yield at last,
And, weakened by many a ghastly wound, fainting, he fell upon the
ground.
But e'er the spark of life had fled, he rose as if up from the dead,
And once more raised his axe on high. Then rang his last fierce
battle cry.
Down fell the axe with his last stroke, the well-tried blade was
shattered and broke.
Our chieftain fell to rise no more, and his life blood oozed from
every pore;
Silent he lay upon the plain, mingling his blood with the foeman's
slain.

"When we beheld our leader fall, a frenzied shout rose from us all.
To save our chief from ruthless hands, from the mad invaders of
our lands,
Caused round our chieftain's lifeless form to fiercely rage the battle
storm.
The wounded braves, in death's last throes, would cast the spear or
draw a bow—
Our shattered ranks were fading fast, they could not stand the awful
blast.
We bore our chieftain's form away — it was suicide to longer stay;
We laid him gently on the ground, in his last sleep and profound.
Once wore we engaged in the strife — once more to battle for our
life;
With weakened hands and failing heart, we cast poisoned spear and
deadly dart.
Eighty-five braves were lying dead, the blood-stained earth their
only bed.
We all must perish here tonight or save ourselves by instant flight,

A weak spot in the foeman's ranks, where death had played its direst pranks,
From where I stood I now espied, and calling my comrades to my side
I bade them quickly follow me, in one grand dash for liberty.
I raised my glittering blade on high, and burst forth once more in battle cry.
With wild yell and fearful bound, my feet scarce seemed to touch the ground;
I broke their ranks and gained the wood and for a moment there I stood.
I saw my friends struggling for life against a host in deadly strife;
At last they fell to rise no more, more ghastly piles of flesh and gore.

"Up yonder rugged mountain side with rapid pace I quickly hied
And upon a beetling rock I stood, gazing upon the angry flood.
Between the dark clouds the moon shone out, throwing its silver light about;
The wind still blew with angry roar, the angry waves still reached the shore;
From far away I soon espied the raft upon the angry tide.
Each moment some high wave hurried a victim to its grave.
I saw a giant wave arise whose crest towered to the skies;
Nearer it came upon its way like hungry wolves in search of prey —
Nearer, still nearer it came, pursuing close its human game.
Each seemed to feel their hour was nigh, that in the deep they soon must die.
The wave came down with thundering sound, a cloud of spray was strewn around,
I heard a wail of fell despair borne away on the midnight air
Oh, what a sight now met my view — the raft that bore that precious crew
Was scattered in fragments far and wide and tossing upon the angry tide.
Overwhelmed with sorrow and woe, to leave this world I longed to go
To join my friends in the land afar, in their bright homes on some twinkling star.
But the Great Spirit willed it so that I must tarry here below,
To be a scourge to our foes, the wild Cheyennes and Arapahoes.
                    .   .   .   .   .

101

"Since that dark night when the storm king did to us such misery
 bring,
When night her mantle has thrown around the silent forms of earth
 and ground,
Ghosts of the warriors slain rise up on their graves again;
Again in battle line they stand, the dead chief leading his command.
But at the first faint streak of day these ghostly forms will fade away.
Behold this lock — now seen so white — in one short hour was
 changed that night.
My time is short on earth below, to a happy home I soon must go.
No happy moments have I passed since Cheikiwow breathed his last,
Only when in the fight I stood, my hands drenched in my foeman's
 blood.
Our chief, Black Eagle, slumbers now with a glorious wreath upon
 his brow,
He fell with many of his band, fighting for home and native land.
My term of life will soon be past — each day I look to be the last —
I long to leave this cumbrous clay and speed afar to endless sky."
                The chieftain ceased, his tale was told
                Of scenes that happened in days of old,
                And night had settled on lake and plain
                When we returned to our camp again.

From *Sons of Colorado*, Vol. I, No. 1 (Denver, June, 1906), pp. 6-8.

CHIPETA'S RIDE

By *John W. Taylor*

Chipeta, wife of the great Ute chieftain, Ouray, aided her husband's pacification policy. Those who knew her, report that she
married Ouray when she was sixteen, in 1859, and stayed with his
people even after his death, in 1880, and after they were removed
to a reservation in Utah. The Ute War, which she helped quell, took
place in 1879. Although historians doubt the authenticity of the
legend of Chipeta's ride, they testify that she did take into her home
the rescued Meeker women and ministered to their needs.

        From mountains covered deep with snow,
        Uncompahgre's clear, bright waters flow,

Down which they plunge, leap and surge and roar,
Then on they sweep by a cabin door,
Where once dwelt Ouray, the king of the land
With Chipeta, his queen, brave and grand.
This brave, wise chief, and his Wild West queen,
Here lived and loved in that home serene.

The setting sun in the golden west,
Had said "Good night" to this home so blessed,
A silence hangs o'er that darkened vale,
Is broken by hoofbeats on the trail,
A weary horse flecked with dust and foam,
Staggers, falls dead, at this chieftain's home,
A courier from the dead steed sprang —
His words in the ear of the chief rang:

"Thornburg and most of his men are slain!
Meeker and his men lie dead on the plain!
The survivors led by Captain Payne,
Whose name should adorn the scroll of fame —
Behind great piles of dead horses lie,
If help comes not soon those boys will die!
Shots fired from the guns of Colorow's braves
Are fast sending them to Wild West graves.

"The four fair women of Meeker's land,
Are captives of Douglas and his band,
Who in passion vile, with cruel hands
Will wrest from them virtue God demands.
A thousand miners in yon high hills,
Their cries for vengeance all this land now fills,
If men who behind those horses lie,
By bullets shot by red hands should die.

"Or should those white women be defiled
To satisfy lust of brutes so wild,
Not a Ute will live to tell the tale,
Or chase the deer o'er mountain trail."

At the words the Chief from his couch then sprang,
His words through the silent night then rang —
"Bring my horse, I ride to stop this fight,
I will be there by tomorrow night."
Quick reached for his gun, shining and bright,
That had served him in many a fight.

Bright's dreaded disease he long had bore,
And would have fallen to the floor
Had not his queen caught him in her arms,
With loving words with which woman charms
Gently bore him to his bear skin bed.

"My dear Chipeta," he faintly said,
"A message from Ouray you must take,
To Colorow before it is too late,
Tell him not another gun to fire,
Or the Utes will meet with vengeance dire!"
"To serve thee, Ouray, I'd ride through fire,
Thy wish is ever my great desire."

With the proud step of her graceful race,
See her move, quickly from place to place,
Now she stands attired in humble pride,
In all the wild grandeur of her tribe,
"I'll go, brave chief, I am ready now."
Placed her red lips to his noble brow.

Like a fawn into the dark, she ran,
Her eager cry was "Sultan! Sultan!"
A chestnut horse with flowing mane
That well loved her call, swift to her came.
Quickly she bridled and saddled him,
That mountain horse, fleet of hoof and limb,
Then, she lightly to the saddle sprung,
From which the horn of Shavano hung.

Oh I wish you could have seen her there,
To her waist hung braids of long black hair,
Her slender form was a sculptor's dream,

Her soft dreamy eyes, a poet's theme,
Alone, brave, ready to make the ride,
To that land where raged the battle tide,
Her dark eyes raised to the sky to pray,
The good Lord to guide her on the way.

Women who walk in city's bright light,
On that dark night would have died of fright,
Not so, this our heroine of the west,
For with courage grand she was possessed,
She slacked her reins, Sultan bounded to the trail,
That once led down Uncompahgre's vale,
Along the gliding shining river,
Born in the land of gold and silver.

Now she rides where naught but cactus grow,
A sound she hears, 'tis a river's flow,
Gunnison's waters before them roar,
They must swim to reach the farther shore,
Now rides where deep, swift, wild waters wave,
Her hand is the helm, his limb the oar,
A boat they glide to the other shore.

She leaps from horse to give him rest,
For thirty miles he has done his best,
Precious is her time, she must not wait,
On, on, she rides at a rapid gait,
Through lands, then in a wild desert state,
Now the sweet homes of a people great,
Where Eckert and Cedaredge now stand,
Then up they rush to the higher land.

The horse brave of heart, and fleet of limb,
Still flies on a mountain crest to win,
See him climb to high Grand Mesa's rim,
And on its top they stop to view now,
Leon Lake's waters, deep, dark and blue,
The stars above reflected there,
Are a wonderous sight her soul to stir,
Enthralled as a poet in a dream,

Her dark eyes are fixed upon the scene —
Its wonderous beauty fills her soul,
But on she must ride to reach her goal.

Sultan gallops down a winding stream,
That flows through primeval forest green,
To where Colorado's waters flow,
Which are children of their mother snow,
From that river bank so high and steep,
They into the seething waters leap,
And they swim across those waters wide,
And land safely on the other side.

Rider and horse are feeling the strain
Of that ride over mountain and plain,
The saddle she takes from her tired steed,
And turns him loose on the grass to feed —
Forty more miles she must ride today
And finish the trip without delay.

In five hours she gallops over the space,
A terrible sight she now does face,
Chief Douglas, a fair young girl has bound,
Is dragging her over the rough ground,
Up the hill to his gray deer skin tent,
Hill and valley with her shrieks are rent,
A rider and horse fly to her side,
And the brave western heroine cried —

"This sweet girl now is one of our tribe,
For I do adopt her as my child,
She and all these women are now free,
And home I will take the four with me."

Three loud blasts from her horn she then blew,
Which startled hills, vales and mountains too,
A minute more, Colorow and his band,
Of four hundred painted warriors stand,

106

Around their lovely queen brave and grand,
All these watch the movement of her hand,
With which she gives Ouray's last command.

Silent and still these dark warriors proud,
Vanish from sight as a passing cloud,
And never again their shouts will fill,
With echoes, mountain valley or hill.
Then into the canon she took her way,
Where piles of dead men and horses lay,
A blast from her horn, sounds loud and clear,
Is heard by brave Payne, the pioneer,
He and his men climb over the dead
Behind which for days they've fought and bled —
Beheld the Ute queen lovely and brave,
Who had ridden far, their lives to save.

From their breast burst forth a mighty cheer,
That swept through the canon far and near,
For that woman of a savage race,
Whose history has the proudest place,
Among heroines whose names are placed
Upon the enduring scroll of fame.

Of all her heroic deeds the grandest
Was to give up the home she possessed,
When the Utes were driven from their land,
A sorrowing, lonely, homeless band.
Then devote to them, her precious life,
Away from dead Ouray, yet his loyal wife.

In a land she never loved, she died,
Neglected, poor, no friend at her side,
When daughters of men of nobles fame,
Who fought with Washington, freedom to gain,
Their souls aglow with patriot fires,
Inherited from their gallant sires,
Erected a tomb near Ouray's shrine,
Where Uncompahgre's bright waters sing,
Then brought her body from Utah's land,

And placed it in that Mausoleum grand,
Where in peaceful sleep it is at rest,
In our own dear land she loved the best.

I tell this tale, as she told it to me,
In the year of eighteen ninety three.

From an unidentified newspaper clipping, a copy of which was given to the editor by Elmo Scott Watson.

CHIPETA

By Eugene Field

As a newspaper versifier, Field was anxious to capitalize on local color, whether sentimental or humorous. In adopting western attitudes during his brief and prankish Denver career, he admitted there was one good Indian who wasn't dead. The following tribute was read at the Third Annual Meeting of the Colorado Press Association, July 11, 1882, by Field, then managing editor of the Denver *Tribune*.

She is bravest and best of a cursed race —
    Give her a lodge on the mountain side,
    And, when she is gone, on a hill provide
The Queen of the Utes' last resting place.

She rode where old Ouray dare not ride —
    A path through the wilderness, rough and wild,
    She rode to plead for woman and child —
She rode by the yawning chasm's side;

She rode on the rocky, fir-clad hill
    Where the panther mewed and the crested jay
    Piped echoless through the desert day —
She rode in the valleys dark and chill.

Oh, such a ride as woman can —
    By the Godlike pow'r that in her lies,
    Or an inspiration from the skies —
Achieve for woman and son of man.

They live, and thro' the country wide —
    Where'er they come, where'er they go,
    Though their hairs grow white as the wintry snow —
They will tell of brave Chipeta's ride!

She is bravest and best of a cursed race —
    Give her a lodge on the mountain side,
    And, when she is gone, on the hill provide
The Queen of the Utes' last resting place.

But give her a page in history, too,
    Though she be rotting in humble shrouds,
    And write on the whitest of God's white clouds
Chipeta's name in eternal blue.

The Daily Rocky Mountain News, Denver, July 12, 1882.

THE CLIFF DWELLING

By Arthur W. Monroe

The natural castles of an early Indian people, in Mesa Verde National Park, remain to awe the white man.

Sleep in your silent glory,
    Dream of days gone by;
Let crumbled walls tell your story,
    And the wind be your lullaby.

Breathe not a word of the past,
    Nor tell the things you know,
But sleep through endless ages,
    O'er the canyon's depth below.

Echo no more the war whoop
    Of your ancient master's voice,
But ever sleep in your mystery,
    And in your silence rejoice.

Arthur W. Monroe, *Sunshine and Shadows* (Montrose, Colorado: The Press Printing Co., n.d.), p. 22. Reprinted by special permission of the author.

HOMES OF THE CLIFF DWELLERS
Headlands of Hoven-Weep

By Stanley Wood

Stanley Wood, editor of Colorado's pioneering regional magazine, *The Great Divide*, from 1889 to 1894, and a leader in the effort to have Mesa Verde supported as a national park, modeled his praise of the pre-historic ruins on Algernon Charles Swinburne's "A Foresaken Garden."

In the sad Southwest, in the mystical Sunland,
 Far from the toil and the turmoil of gain;
Hid in the heart of the only — the one land
 Beloved of the Sun, and bereft of the rain;
The one weird land where the wild winds blowing,
 Sweep with a wail o'er the plains of the dead,
A ruin ancient beyond all knowing,
 Rears its head.

On the cañon's side, in the ample hollow,
 That the keen winds carved in ages past,
The Castle walls, like the nest of a swallow,
 Have clung and have crumbled to this at last.
The ages since man's foot has rested
 Within these walls, no man may know;
For here the fierce grey eagle nested
 Long ago.

Above those walls the crags lean over,
 Below, they dip to the river's bed;
Between, fierce-winged creatures hover;
 Beyond, the plain's wild waste is spread.
No foot has climbed the pathway dizzy,
 That crawls away from the blasted heath,
Since last it felt the ever busy
 Foot of Death.

In that haunted Castle — it must be haunted,
 For men have lived here, and men have died,

And maidens loved, and lovers daunted,
    Have hoped and feared, have laughed and sighed —
In that haunted Castle the dust has drifted,
    But the eagles only may hope to see
What shattered Shrines and what Altars rifted,
    There may be.

The white, bright rays of the sunbeam sought it;
    The cold, clear light of the moon fell here;
The west wind sighed, and the south wind brought it
    Songs of Summer year after year.
Runes of Summer, but mute and runeless,
    The Castle stood; no voice was heard,
Save the harsh, discordant, wild and tuneless
    Cry of bird.

The spring rains poured, and the torrent rifted
    A deeper way — the foam-flakes fell,
Held for a moment poised and lifted,
    Down to a fiercer whirlpool's hell.
On the Castle tower no guard, in wonder,
    Paused in his marching to and fro,
For on the turret the mighty thunder
    Found no foe.

No voice of Spring — no Summer glories
    May wake the warders from their sleep,
Their graves are made by the sad Dolores,
    And the barren headlands of Hoven-weep.
Their graves are nameless — their race forgotten,
    Their deeds, their words, their fate, are one
With the mist, long ages past begotten,
    Of the Sun.

Those castled cliffs they made their dwelling;
    They lived and loved, they fought and fell;
No faint, far voice comes to us telling
    More than those crumbling walls can tell.

They lived their life, their fate fulfilling,
    Then drew their last faint, faltering breath,
Their hearts congealed, clutched by the chilling
    Hand of Death.

Dismantled towers, and turrets broken,
    Like grim and war-worn braves who keep
A silent guard, with grief unspoken
    Watch o'er the graves by the Hoven-weep.
The nameless graves of a race forgotten;
    Whose deeds, whose words, whose fate are one
With the mist, long ages past begotten,
    Of the Sun.

Reprinted from *Rhymes of the Rockies, or What Poets Have Found to Say of the Beautiful Scenery on the Denver and Rio Grande Railroad* (Chicago: Poole Brothers, Printers and Engravers, 1887; 11th edition, 1893), pp. 34-35.

THE WAR DANCE

By Robert V. Carr

Before free verse was widely used, one writer tried to reproduce Indian rhythms in the white man's metre and rhyme.

Bodies that gleam like rare bronze in the fire,
Voices that chant of an ancient desire;
Leaping and gliding and telling a story,
Weaving in pantomime figures of glory.
Bending and crouching in postures of grace,
Stamping and circling in rhythmical pace,
To stolid drum's tunking and unchanging beat,
As autumn leaves blown drift the young warriors' feet;
For to-morrow they follow on fair Danger's trail,
And to-morrow — to-morrow the women will wail.

Robert V. Carr, *Cowboy Lyrics* (Privately printed, 1908; Boston: Small, Maynard & Co., 1912), p. 193.

THE WESTERN TRAIL
A Sioux Version

By Robert V. Carr

Carr was moved, early, into cadenced lines, apparently by the influence of Indian oratory.

In the beginning the Great Spirit gave the prairie rare gifts:
The mirage, the warm rains of springtime, the grasses and the flowers;
The buffalo, the village by the river and the children basking in the sun.
Happy were we then, O, my people!
But from the East a white warrior came and with a mighty arrow wounded the prairie;
And the grasses and the flowers withered and the herds and villages melted away —
Melted, O, my people! as the snow melts before the Chinook.
In time the wound healed, but a scar was left — a long, white scar across the prairie's breast.

Robert V. Carr, *Black Hills Ballads* (Denver: The Reed Publishing Co., 1902), p. 123.

THE RED GHOSTS CHANT

By Lilian White Spencer

The Ute finally comes into his own as an influence and inspiration for a modern Colorado poet in the following chant.

> We are sons of mighty Manitou.
> Our mother is his child, Hi-yu!
> Our father is the Bear, Hi-ya!
> We have tipis in the sky and are
> Above all other tribes, Hi-yu!
> We are brothers to the hills, Hi-ya!
> We can climb and reach the evening star.
> Let us shuffle, let us stamp, Hi-yu!
> Let us dance to mighty Manitou!

All the Utes are brave and strong, Hi-ya!
Utes are eagles flying high and far . . . . .
Hi-yu! Hi-yu! Hi-yu! Hi-ya!!!

Lilian White Spencer, *Arrowheads* (New York: The Parade Publishing Co., 1929), p. 20. Reprinted by special permission of the author.

MOUNTAIN LIARS

By Ann Woodbury Hafen

For the sake of a story, terse-talking Jim Bridger is made a boasting liar. But the roughness of the prank is true to the spirit of the Indian-like "mountain men."

I

Swapping yarns, two Mountain Men
 Chewed and spat in the fire;
Trying to prove to the trapper band —
 Who was the bigger liar?

"I seed a crystial mountain onct
 With foothills, all of bones
From flyin' birds it bumped to death!"
 Jim Bridger sagely owns.

"Gar! I seed a ice-cold river, pard,
 What runs down hill so fast
The water gets so all-fired hot
 It cooks the mountain bass,"

Jim Baker vowed. But Bridger met
 That tale with mounting scorn:
"You brags of 'putrified forests' too.
 But long 'fore you was born

"I seed a tree half peetrified,
 Half growin' green and strong;
And in its limbs a peetrified bird
 Was singin' a peetrified song!

114

"Behind this tree was a chasm where
    I loped onct, over the brink
And believe this beaver kitten, boys,
    I didn't noways sink.

"Acrost that canyon three miles deep
    I rode to tother side
And landed safe, for durn my skin,
    That *air* was peetrified!"

    The boys guffawed and slapped their thighs.
        While Baker poked the fire,
    They all allowed Jim Bridger was
        The West's "gol-durndest liar."

II

Jim Baker never liked to be
    Wiped up by any one,
"Gar! I kin outdo Bridger thar —
    Out-spit, out-fight, out-run,

"Out-everything except his sass!"
    He raised a smeary hand
And swore in trapper-Injun style
    He'd show the mountain band.

Next morning Baker, hunting wood,
    Rushed back to camp pell-mell,
"Two bear-cubs, Jim. I dares ye, pard,
    To wrestle 'em a spell.

"With nary help, let's skulp the varmints
    With a skinnin' knife,
I cain't out-fib ye, Bridger, but
    Out-fight ye — bet yer life!"

With shooting-irons left behind,
    Each man attacked his cub.
The varmints stood upright and sparred,
    They seemed intent to rub

115

These upstarts off from Mother Earth.
    Young Baker did not know
These bears had trained for this-here bout
    Some million years ago.

To left and right he jabbed his knife
    Intending mortal wound.
The cub's forelegs were streaming blood
    And from its throat a sound

Of hideous grief — the age-old cry
    Of young one for the dam.
A fear upset the Mountain Men.
    This fight they thought a sham

Might turn them both to buzzard's meat
    Avenged by Mother Bear.
The cubs and trappers gripped to clinch.
    With free arm in the air

Jim Baker sank his hungry knife
    Downward through the ribs.
The death-hug loosed. The fight was won—
    Avenged were spineless fibs!

Jim Bridger still was slashing wild
    And cursing like a Sioux.
That cub was too affectionate.
    Could Bridger count his coup?

Young Baker watched and gloated. Gar!
    That night around the fire
He sure would brag he wrastled cubs
    And beat the mountain liar.

"Help, Baker, help!" Though oozing blood
    He rushed to join the spree.
He grappled Bridger's maddened cub—
    While Bridger climbed a tree!

Home went the knife as a razor claw
    Gouged Baker's battered face —
His iron hands had skulped two cubs
    And won the bloody race.

Two skins were his to show the boys,
    And one fine bloomin' eye!
He started! From a distant tree
    Came Bridger's warning cry!

"Hey! Hoof it, Baker! Git yer gun!
    Here comes Mother Bruin!"
He lunged to fetch his shooting stick,
    Scarce knowin' what he's doin'

And stumbled back where Bridger grinned
    In safety from the tree,
"Whar is that she-bear?" Baker gasped,
    "My busted eye don't see!"

Then Bridger, plum ashamed, climbed down
    And helped his pal to camp,
"You fightin' fool, you clean forgot
    How I'm the lyin' champ!"

Ann Woodbury Hafen, Quenched Fire (Denver: The World Press, 1937), pp. 13-16. Reprinted by special permission of the author.

THE OLD SCOUT'S LAMENT

By Captain William F. Drannan

One of the last of the scouts said goodbye to the frontier in these verses, at the conclusion of his book of reminiscences.

Come all of you, my brother scouts,
    And join me in my song;
Come, let us sing together,
    Though the shadows fall so long.

Of all the old frontiersmen,
 That used to scour the plain,
There are but very few of them
 That with us yet remain.

Day after day, they're dropping off;
 They are going, one by one;
Our clan is fast decreasing;
 Our race is almost run.

There were many of our number
 That never wore the blue,
But, faithfully they did their part,
 As brave men, tried and true.

They never joined the army,
 But had other work to do
In piloting the coming folks,
 To help them safely through.

But brothers, we are failing;
 Our race is almost run;
The days of elk and buffalo,
 And beaver traps, are gone.

Oh! the days of elk and buffalo,
 It fills my heart with pain
To know those days are passed and gone,
 To never come again.

We fought the red-skin rascals
 Over valley, hill and plain;
We fought him to the mountain top,
 And fought him down again.

Those fighting days are over;
 The Indian yell resounds
No more along the border;
 Peace sends far sweeter sounds.

But we found great joy, old comrades,
   To hear and make it die,
We won bright homes for gentle ones,
   And now, our West, good-bye.

Captain William F. Drannan, *Thirty-One Years on the Plains and in the Mountains* (Chicago: Thomas W. Jackson Publishing Co., 1900), pp. 653-654.

KIT CARSON'S LAST SMOKE

By Stanley Vestal

The scout has passed into heroic legend, celebrated in the following ballad by a twentieth century poet-scholar.

Kit Carson came to old Fort Lyons
Sick as he could be:
"Make me a bed of buffalo robes
On the floor in the corner," says he;

"Make me a bed of buffalo robes
Like we used along the trail;
I thought to ha' lived for a hundred year,
But my heart is beginning to fail;

"I ought to ha' lived for a hundred year,
But the strength in my legs is done;
I swelled the veins in them long ago
When the Blackfoot made me run.

"Take care of my children, *compadre*,
I've taken my last ride;
Bury my bones in good old Taos
By my dear Josephine's side.

"I leave you my Cross-J cattle,
My house and ranch, and the rest;
Tell Wiggins, and Tom, and the Carson men
That I always loved them best.

"Now cook me some first-rate doin's —
I'm tired of this sick man's feed;
A buffalo steak and a bowl of coffee
And a pipe are what I need."

The Army doctor shook his head
And looked Kit in the eye:
"General, now, you ought to know,
If you eat that meal you'll die!"

"I never was scairt of death," says Kit;
His eye was cold and blue;
"I've faced it many's the time," he said;
They knew his words were true.

"There war times when the Injuns bested me;
There war times when I run like sin;
But I never took fright of a square meal yet,
And it's too late now to begin.

"I'd ruther die on my pins," Kit said,
"With the bull meat under my belt,
Than to die in my bed by inches
Like a beaver trapped for his pelt."

They brought him a big thick buffalo steak:
He ate it every bite.
He smacked his lips when he drank the coffee,
And swore it tasted right.

"Will you have your meershaum, General,
Or your Cheyenne calumet?
Will you have the pipe that Frémont gave,
Or what pipe shall we get?"

"Get me my old black clay, Sherrick;
Give me my old dudheen;
It has been over many a trail with me;
It has seen what I have seen."

He packed the baccy in the bowl,
Inhaled the smoke so blue;
A happy smile spread o'er his face —
That face so bold and true.

He smoked the pipe out to the end
And brushed the ashes off.
Then Death (whose bullets could not kill)
Killed Kit with a little cough.

The ladies of that lonely post
That loved him one and all;
One gave her satin wedding-gown
To line his coffin-wall.

The ladies on that winter day
For love of one so brave
Pulled from their bonnets all the flowers
To strew upon his grave.

He was happy when he died,
And brave and true alive.
God send the West a many such
To make our country thrive!

Stanley Vestal, *Fandango: Ballads of the Old West* (Boston: Houghton Mifflin Co., 1927), pp. 63-66. Reprinted by special permission of the author and the publisher.

LARAMIE TRAIL

By Joseph Mills Hanson

From the establishment of Fort Laramie as a trading post in 1834, trails went out from it like spokes from a hub. It became an army post in 1849 and from then until the end of the Indian wars "the boys in blue," four by four, rode forth from this army post against warring Indians and lawbreakers, in our Army's longest war. Many of their saddles came back empty.

Across the crests of the naked hills,
  Smooth-swept by the winds of God,
It cleaves its way life a shaft of gray,
  Close-bound by the prairie sod.
It stretches flat from the sluggish Platte
  To the lands of forest shade;
The clean trail, the lean trail,
  The trail the troopers made.

It draws aside with a wary curve
  From the lurking, dark ravine,
It launches fair as a lance in air
  O'er the raw-ribbed ridge between;
With never a wait it plunges straight
  Through river or reed-grown brook;
The deep trail, the steep trail,
  The trail the squadrons took.

They carved it well, these men of old,
  Stern lords of the border war,
They wrought it out with their sabres stout
  And marked it with their gore.
They made it stand as an iron band
  Along the wild frontier;
The strong trail, the long trail,
  The trail of force and fear.

For the stirring note of the bugle's throat
  Ye may hark to-day in vain,
For the track is scarred by the gang-plow's shard
  And gulfed in the growing grain.
But wait to-night for the moonrise white;
  Perchance ye may see them tread
The lost trail, the ghost trail,
  The trail of the gallant dead.

'Twixt cloud and cloud o'er the pallid moon
  From the nether dark they glide
And the grasses sigh as they rustle by
  Their phantom steeds astride.

By four and four as they rode of yore
    And well they know the way;
The dim trail, the grim trail,
    The trail of toil and fray.

With tattered guidons spectral thin
    Above their swaying ranks,
With carbines swung and sabres slung
    And the gray dust on their flanks.
They march again as they marched it then
    When the red men dogged their track,
The gloom trail, the doom trail,
    The trail they came not back.

They pass, like a flutter of drifting fog,
    As the hostile tribes have passed,
As the wild-wing'd birds and the bison herds
    And the unfenced prairies vast,
And those who gain by their strife and pain
    Forget, in the land they won,
The red trail, the dead trail,
    The trail of duty done.

But to him who loves heroic deeds
    The far-flung path still bides,
The bullet sings and the war-whoop rings
    And the stalwart trooper rides.
For they were the sort from Snelling Fort
    Who traveled fearlessly
The bold trail, the old trail,
    The trail to Laramie.

Joseph Mills Hanson, *Frontier Ballads* (Chicago: A. C. McClurg & Co., 1910), pp. 40-41.

THE DEATH OF CUSTER

By Captain Jack Crawford.

Poet-scout Crawford explained the origin of this poem as follows: "In July, 1876, I received a telegram from W. F. Cody (Buffalo Bill), which read: 'Have you heard of the death of our brave Custer?' I immediately wrote the following verses, which I sent Mr. Cody, in answer to his dispatch, on the following day."

Did I hear the news from Custer?
 Well I reckon I did, old pard;
It came like a streak of lightnin',
 And, you bet, it hit me hard.
I ain't no hand to blubber,
 And the briny ain't run for years;
But chalk me down for a lubber,
 If I didn't shed regular tears.

What for? Now look ye here, Bill,
 You're a bully boy, that's true;
As good as e'er wore buckskin,
 Or fought with the boys in blue;
But I'll bet my bottom dollar
 Ye had no trouble to muster
A tear, or perhaps a hundred,
 When ye heard of the death of Custer.

He always thought well of you, pard,
 And had it been Heaven's will,
In a few more days you'd met him,
 And he'd welcomed his old scout, Bill.
For, if ye remember, at Hat Creek
 I met ye with General Carr;
We talked of the brave young Custer,
 And recounted his deeds of war.

But little we knew even then, pard
 (And that's just two weeks ago,
How little we dreamed of disaster,
 Or that he had met the foe) —

124

That the fearless, reckless hero,
    So loved by the whole frontier,
Had died on the field of battle
    In this our centennial year.

I served with him in the army
    In the darkest days of the war;
And I reckon ye know his record,
    For he was our guiding star.
And the boys who gathered round him
    To charge in the early morn,
War just like the brave who perished
    With him on the Little Horn.

And where is the satisfaction,
    And how are we going to get square?
By giving the Reds more rifles?
    Invite them to take more hair?
We want no scouts, no trappers,
    Nor men who know the frontier?
Phil, old boy, you're mistaken —
    You must have the volunteer.

They talk about peace with these demons
    By feeding and clothing them well;
I'd as soon think an angel from heaven
    Would reign with contentment in hell;
And some day these Quakers will answer
    Before the great Judge of us all,
For the death of our daring young Custer,
    And the boys who around him did fall.

Perhaps I am judging them harshly,
    But I mean what I'm telling ye, pard;
I'm letting them down mighty easy —
    Perhaps they may think it is hard.
But I tell ye the day is approaching —
    The boys are beginning to muster,
That day of the great retribution —
    The day of revenge for our Custer.

And I will be with you, friend Cody,
    My mite will go in with the boys;
I shared all their hardships last winter,
    I shared all their sorrows and joys;
So tell them I'm coming, friend William,
    I trust I will meet you ere long;
Regards to the boys in the mountains,
    Yours truly, in friendship still strong.

Capt. Jack Crawford, *The Poet Scout* (San Francisco: H. Keller & Co., 1879; New York: Funk and Wagnalls, 1886), pp. 106-108.

MILES KEOGH'S HORSE

By John Hay

Eight years after *Pike Country Ballads* (1871), the statesman and poet John Hay was inspired to verse by General Order No. 7, issued on April 10, 1878, by Colonel Sturgis, pensioning for life "the only living representative of the bloody tragedy of the Little Big Horn, Montana, June 25, 1876." Captain Keogh commanded troop I of the 7th Calvary. The horse died in 1891, aged 31, and was "set up in life-like shape" in the Dyche Museum at the University of Kansas, Lawrence, Kansas.

On the bluff of the Little Big Horn
    At the close of a woeful day,
Custer and his three hundred
    In death and silence lay.

Three hundred to three thousand!
    They had bravely fought and bled;
For such is the will of Congress
    When the White Man meets the Red.

The White Men are ten millions,
    The thriftiest under the sun;
The Reds are fifty thousand,
    And warriors every one.

126

So Custer and all his fighting men
　　Lay under the evening skies,
Staring up at the tranquil heaven
　　With wide, accusing eyes.

And of all that stood at noonday
　　In that fiery scorpion ring,
Miles Keogh's horse at evening
　　Was the only living thing.

Alone from that field of slaughter,
　　Where lay the three hundred slain,
The horse Comanche wandered,
　　With Keogh's blood on his mane.

And Sturgis issued this order,
　　Which future times shall read,
While the love and honor of comrades
　　Are the soul of the soldier's creed.

He said:
Let the horse Comanche,
　　Henceforth till he shall die,
Be kindly cherished and cared for
　　By the Seventh Cavalry.

He shall do no labor; he shall never know
　　The touch of spur or rein;
Nor shall his back be ever crossed
　　By living rider again.

And at regimental formation
　　Of the Seventh Cavalry,
Comanche, draped in mourning and led
　　By a trooper of Company I,
Shall parade with the regiment!

　　　　　　　　　　　Thus it was
　　Commanded, and thus done,
By order of General Sturgis, signed
　　By Adjutant Carlington.

Even as the sword of Custer,
   In his disastrous fall,
Flashed out a blaze that charmed the world
   And glorified his pall,

This order, issued amid the gloom
   That shrouds our Army's name,
When all foul beasts are free to rend
   And tear its honest fame,

Shall prove to a callous people
   That the sense of a soldier's worth,
That the love of comrades, the honor of arms,
   Have not yet perished from earth.

Poems by John Hay (Boston: Houghton Mifflin Co., 1890), pp. 97
101.

THE SPRINGFIELD CALIBRE FIFTY

By Joseph Mills Hanson

At the suggestion of Master Armorer E. Allin, the War Department in 1866 converted its stock of muzzle loading muskets into breech loaders. A tube was brazed inside the barrels, reducing the bore from .58 to .50. This weapon, here celebrated in Kiplingesque verse, helped turn the tide against the redmen after their "Bloody Year on the Plains" of 1865.

I was wrought of walnut blocks and rolled rod steel,
   I was hammered, lathed, and mandrelled, stock and plate,
I was gauged and tested, bayonet to heel,
   Then shipped for service, twenty in a crate.

      For I was the calibre fifty,
         Hi! — dough-boys, you haven't forgot
      The click of my tumblers shifty
         And the kick of the butt when I shot?
      I was nothing too light on your shoulder,
         You were glad when you stacked me o' nights,

But I'd drill an Apach'
From the thousand-yard scratch
If you'd only hold straight on the sights —old sights!
My trusty old Buffington sights!

In oil-soaked chests at Watervliet I've laid,
I have rusted in Vancouver through the rains,
I have scorched on Fort Mohave's baked parade,
And caked with sand at Sedgwick on the plains.

For I led every march on the border,
And I taught every rookie to fight;
Though he'd curse me in close marching order,
Lord! — he'd hug me on picket at night
As he thought of the herd-guard at Buford
When Sitting Bull swooped within reach,
And 'twas every man's life,
It was bullet and knife
Had my cartridges jammed in the breech — lock breech!
In my solid block, hammer-lock breech!

It was I who lashed the Modocs from their lair
With Wheaton in the Tule Lava Bed;
It was I who drove Chief Joseph to despair
When I streaked the slopes of Bear Paw with his dead.

For I was a proof most impressive —
The Springfield the infantry bore —
To redskins with spirits aggressive
That peace is more healthful than war;
I showed them on Musselshell River
And again, yet more plain, at Slim Butte;
They were plucky as sin
But they had to come in
When they found how the Springfield could shoot —
shoot, shoot!
How my blue bottle barrel could shoot!

I was Vengeance when, with Miles through trackless snow,
    The "fighting Fifth" took toll for Custer's fall;
I was Justice when we flayed Geronimo;
    I was Mercy to the famished horde of Gall.

        Oh, I was slow-plodding and steady;
            Not hot, like the carbine, to raid,
        But when he found trouble too ready
            He was glad for his big brother's aid;
        For sometimes he'd scatter the outposts,
            Then wait, if the foe proved too stout,
                Till, at "Front into line!"
                It was business of mine
        While the infantry volleyed the rout — rout, rout!
        While I cleared out the village in rout!

But those years have sped; long silent are my lips;
    Now my sturdy grandson rules the host I knew,
And a drab-clad army trusts his five-shell clips
    As of old the blue-clad held my one shot true.

        Still my dotage takes solace of glory
            From my turbulent youth and its scenes.
        As vivid with valorous story
            As the isles of the far Philippines.
        Though the steel-jacket smokeless is sovereign
            And I'm proud of my name on his crest,
                It was black smoke and lead
                When the skirmish lines spread
        With the Springfield that conquered the West —
                West, West!
        With the hard-fighting arm of the West!

Joseph Mills Hanson, *Frontier Ballads* (Chicago: A. C. McClurg &
Co., 1910), pp. 25-27.

THE INDIAN GHOST DANCE AND WAR

By Pvt. W. H. Prather

Fevered by the Ghost Dance with the hope of regaining their "lost Paradise," the Indians of the Bad Lands met the Army on Wounded Knee Creek in January, 1891. This "classic of the Barracks" was written during the action and later printed and distributed among the soldiers. "Sung to a simple air" with "vigor and expression and a particularly rousing chorus" it became a favorite of frontiersmen of Dakota and Nebraska also.

The Red Skins left their Agency, the Soldiers left their post,
All on the strength of an Indian tale about Messiah's ghost
Got up by savage chieftains to lead their tribes astray;
But Uncle Sam wouldn't have it so, for he ain't built that way.
They swore that this Messiah came to them in vision's sleep,
And promised to restore their game and Buffaloes a heap,
So they must start a big ghost dance, then all would join their band.
And may be so we lead the way into the great Bad Land.
Chorus
They claimed the shirt Messiah gave, no bullet could go through,
But when the Soldiers fired at them they saw this was not true.
The Medicine man supplied them with their great Messiah's grace.
And he, too, pulled his freight and swore the 7th hard of face.
About their tents the Soldiers stood, awaiting one and all,
That they might hear the trumpet clear when sounding General call
Or Boots and Saddles in a rush, that each and every man
Might mount in haste, ride soon and fast to stop this devilish band.
But Generals great like Miles and Brooke don't do things up that way,
For they know an Indian like a book, and let him have his sway
Until they think him far enough and then to John they'll say,
"You had better stop your fooling or we'll bring our guns to play."

The 9th marched out with splendid cheer the Bad Lands to explore —
With Col. Henry at their head they never fear the foe;
So on they rode from Xmas eve 'till dawn of Xmas day;
The Red Skins heard the 9th was near and fled in great dismay;
The 7th is of courage bold both officers and men,
But bad luck seems to follow them and twice has took them in;

131

They came in contact with Big Foot's warriors in their fierce might.
This chief made sure he had a change of vantage in the fight.

A fight took place, 'twas hand to hand, unwarned by trumpet call,
While the Sioux were dropping man by man — the 7th killed them all,
And to that regiment he said "Ye noble braves, well done,
Although you lost some gallant men a glorious fight you've won."
The 8th was there, the 6th rode miles to swell that great command
And waited orders night and day to round up Short Bull's band
The Infantry marched up in mass the Calvary's support,
And while the latter rounded up, the former held the fort.

E battery of the 1st stood by and did their duty well,
For every time the Hotchkiss barked they say a hostile fell.
Some Indian soldiers chipped in too and helped to quell the fray,
And now the campaign's ended and the soldiers marched away.
So all have done their share, you see, whether it was thick or thin,
And all helped break the ghost dance up and drive the hostiles in.
The settlers in that region now can breathe with better grace;
They only ask and pray to God to make John hold his base.

From James Mooney, "The Ghost-Dance Religion and the Sioux Outbreaks of 1890," *14th Report Bureau of Ethnology*, Part 2 (Washington, D. C.: 1896), pp. 883-970.

REMEMBER THE PROMISE, DAKOTAH

By Robert V. Carr

The Ghost Dance rising was an odd offshoot of Christian missions to the Indian. Some of the red men conceived their own, earthly Messiah.

> Remember the promise, Dakotah,
>   Remember Messiah has said:
> "I come on the morrow, my children,
>   And with me the numberless dead.
> Again will the sunlight on lances
>   Shiver and break at the morn —
>
> On the lances of warriors, Dakotah,
>   The bright eagle feathers adorn.
> Again will the buffalo fatten,
>   Again will the swift hunters roam;
> Dance the ghost-dance, O Dakotah!
>   For to-morrow thy people come home."

Robert V. Carr, *Cowboy Lyrics* (Privately printed, 1908; Boston: Small, Maynard & Co., 1912), p. 188.

BEECHER ISLAND

By Arthur Chapman

In 1868 a force under Colonel George A. Forsyth was besieged for a week by Cheyennes and Sioux on an island in the Arickaree Valley on a fork of the Republican River. When Forsyth was successfully relieved, it is said, the power of the Plains Indians was broken. The island was named after Lt. Fred Beecher, who was killed. It was later obliterated when the Republican changed its course.

All's peace to-day at Beecher Isle,
   And cattle stand knee-deep
In that bright stream, once stained with red,
   Where human life was cheap;
No war-whoops echo mile on mile —
All's peace to-day at Beecher Isle.

The lark upon the barren hills
   Once cowered in affright,
When came the horrid clash of arms
   That told of Forsyth's fight;
No more shall foe match wile with wile —
All's peace to-day at Beecher Isle.

The guns that spoke are silent now;
   Keen eyes are closed, alas!
The trail of vanished redskinned hosts
   Is overgrown with grass;
But Memory shall abide the while —
All's peace to-day at Beecher Isle.

Included in Eugene Parsons, *A Guidebook to Colorado* (Boston: Little, Brown and Co., 1911), pp. 339-340. Reprinted by special permission of the copyright holder, Mrs. Kathleen C. Chapman.

IV

FRONTIER DOINGS

THE PIONEER

By Eugene Field

Newspapers were an important and integral part of frontier life. Literary men like Mark Twain and Eugene Field first developed as writers on frontier publications. In return, they created a sometimes humorous but nonetheless pious legend around the pioneers.

Fill up your glass, O comrade true,
　　With sparkling wine that cheers,
And let us drink a bumper to
　　The sturdy pioneers:
The honest men, the women fair,
　　Who, years and years ago,
Had steady hearts and heads to dare
　　Deeds we may never know,
　　Nor page in history show.

They had their uses then, and now
　　They have their uses too,
For oh! they live to tell us how,
　　In eighteen sixty-two
The summer was the hottest time
　　That ever scorched our State,
And then, with earnestness sublime,
　　They hasten to relate
　　Tales vast to contemplate,

And speak of bitter wintry woe.
　　Why, mercy sakes alive!
There fell a fifteen foot of snow
　　In eighteen sixty-five!
Three foot of water in the Platte
　　Was frozen ten foot thick,
And, seeming not content with that,
　　Each man and wife and chick
　　With rheumatiz took sick.

And should we smile? The years gone by
     With martyr lives are strewn;
We're gaily treading, you and I,
     The path which they have hewn,
Hewn from the desert and the mine,
     Posterity to cheer.
Let's toast them in the sparkling wine,
     Drink to the mem'ries dear!
     Drink to the pioneer!

Reprinted from *The Denver Tribune* of January 29,1883.

THE STATIONED SCOUT

By Lyman H. Sproull

The "mountain man," fur trapper and trader, preceded the gold
hunter and settler into the Far West of the Rockies, and later acted
as guide for wagon trains or as pathfinder for the railroad engineers.
In later life, he often learned to his dismay that his enterprise had
helped spread the civilization from which he had fled. Sproull kindly
puts his pathfinder high up above the towns.

High on the bold, gray granite shelf
     He builds his cabin, bleak and lone,
Where eagles well might covet it
     As in an eyrie of their own.

Here from his station on the height
     He views the land far, far below,
And sees where slopes of pinon green
     Reach upward, ending in the snow.

With pipe and glass, and dog and gun,
     Companions of the plain and wood,
He sits and scans the broken peaks,
     Which breathe of peace and solitude.

All thro' the quiet night he hears
　　The weird and lonely owlet hoots;
And at the dawn afar appears
　　The smouldering camp-fire of the Utes.

The blazing disk of morning sun
　　Across the plains, a burning flood,
Lights up his low and dingy room,
　　And paints old Baldy's head with blood.

He sees far on the plains below,
　　With distant hazy dreams endowed,
Each patch of moving buffalo,
　　So like the shadow of a cloud.

Thro' all the heat of summer day,
　　Each change, each object on the plain,
Or in the hills, arrests his eye,
　　Until the shadows grow again.

He sees the western sun sink low,
　　To hide behind the neighboring peaks,
Which feed from fields of shining snow
　　The babbling fountains of the creeks.

And then at night the campers' light
　　Comes dimly on the distant plain,
Which brings to him in memories bright
　　The days of roving youth again.

He sees the crescent 'mid the rift
　　Of nightly clouds, in tranquil light,
Back down along the notched clift
　　To bid the world and him good-night.

Lyman H. Sproull, *Snowy Summits* (St. Louis: A. R. Fleming Printing Co., 1898), pp. 15-17.

THE EMIGRANT'S CHILD

By Lyman H. Sproull

Many died before they reached the gold fields or the homestead lands. Their unmarked graves were the first "roots" put down by emigrant families.

> Far out in the hush of the mountain land
> There lies the grave of a little child;
> Unwept by heart and untended by hand —
> Alone with the grass and the aspen wild.
>
> It was years ago — so the story goes —
> When the "Fifties" rang with the tales of gold,
> That they laid her there, 'mid the falling snows,
> To sleep alone in the damp and cold.
>
> What mother sobbed with the pangs of woe,
> What father grieved as he urged his teams,
> Tradition tells not, and we only know
> That the child is there in a land of dreams.
>
> It was just last year, when I passed that way,
> I saw o'er the mound in the bushes low,
> A bird had erected her nest to stay
> And sing to the soul of the sleeper below.

Lyman H. Sproull, *Snowy Summits* (St. Louis: A. R. Fleming Printing Co., 1898), pp. 27-28.

ROOT HOG OR DIE

By Floyd B. Small

Until the railroads came through, the lifeline of the West for tools, clothing, medicines, weapons, liquor, and much of its food staples was the ox-drawn wagon. Oxen were known as "bulls." The slogan "root hog or die" inspired a popular song of which this poem is a parody.

(Dedicated to the Early Bull Team Freighters. Written by the Author in the Year 1869.)

There was some jolly drivers on the Denver City Line,
From Missouri to the Rockies we drove in sixty-nine;
I drove Bobtail, Duke and Baldy, Buck, Jerry and old Si,
And they all pulled together, for 'twas root hog or die.

I remember how it was when we first went on the road;
The bulls were very awkward, for they had a heavy load.
We could whip and we would holler, if we swore 'twas on the sly;
But we got our teams along, for 'twas root hog or die.

Some may not know what we had to eat;
A dry piece of bread and a dirty piece of meat,
A little old molasses and coffee made from rye,
Beans, if we had them, for 'twas root hog or die.

Every day at noon there was something to do,
If 'twas nothing else, an ox we had to shoe;
With a rope we'd throw him, and there he had to lie
Till the shoes were tacked upon him, for 'twas root hog or die.

There were many strange sights to be seen along the road:
The antelope, and deer and the big horned toad,
The buffalo and elk and the swift antelope that jumped so high;
With all the bloody Indians, 'twas root hog or die.

There were prairie dogs, rattlesnakes and prickly pear,
Screech owls and buffalo bones to be seen everywhere,
With all the dead oxen by the vile alkali,
They were very thick in places where 'twas root hog or die.

Floyd B. Small, *Autobiography of a Pioneer* (Seattle: F. B. Small, 1916), pp. 100-101.

BALDY GREEN

Anonymous

Mail, gold, and people came in and went out of the frontier
towns by stage coach. Western stories have accustomed us to the
notion that being "held up" was an essential part of a coach's run.
Dr. Pound noted that this spirited ballad was heard in 1880 by
Edward Burnett of Buffalo, Wyoming, near where Sheridan, Wyoming, is now. He thought it was composed about 1866-69. "A teacher
of music later transcribed the tune as he sung it."

Come listen to my ditty
'Twill not detain you long
'Tis about one Baldy Green
And I'll tell you in my song.
For he could swing a whip so lightly
That he was sure to shine
He was a way-up six horse driver
On Ben Holladay's stage line.

As Baldy came driving into town
As lively as a coon,
Six men jumped into the middle of the road,
By the pale light of the moon.
The one he caught his leaders
Another his gun he cocks
Says he, "Baldy we're sorry to trouble you
But hand us down that box."

O those leaders they knew Baldy,
And Baldy he knew them.
He whistled to them lightly
And they were off again.
The swing team and the wheelers
Were also full of pride.
They kicked the robbers from them, —
'Twas Baldy Green's last ride.

As the stage coach started down the road,
Those robbers they were mean.
They unlimbered their six shooters
Shot gallant Baldy Green.
When they took Baldy from the seat
With his last breath he told,
"The road agents they've got Baldy,
But Baldy saved the gold."

Louise Pound, "Baldy Green," *Southern Folklore Quarterly*, Vol. 6 (June, 1942), pp. 121-122.

OLD BALAAM

Anonymous

The surefooted mule, or the jackass, carries burdens into the mountains where even narrow gauge spur railroads cannot reach. An unknown bard endowed one of these beasts, "Balaam," of the Signal Corps on Pikes Peak, with a human voice to protest a civil service "cut," some time before 1886.

Where great Pike's Peak his summit rears
'Mid foot-hills robed in richest brown,
And o'er the Great Plains proudly peers —
A monarch he with snowy crown, —
There high above the ocean's tides,
A famed, historic mule resides.

Upon the Peak's supremest height,
Brave men a tireless vigil keep;
'Tis they who, with unerring sight,
Spy storms afar that onward sweep,
And herald to the world below
When sun shall shine or tempest blow.

From plain to mountain's crest there leads,
Round cliff and chasm's brink, a trail;
Sure feet, indeed, the creature needs

Who safe the dizzy heights would scale,
Where one false step the wretch might throw
O'er precipice to death below.

Of all the beasts that climb this trail,
'Tis Balaam (so our mule is named)
Whose history forms the strangest tale,
Whose exploits are so justly famed —
"Old Prob's" most trusty delegate,
For Western things to regulate.

For full eight years has Balaam toiled
This signal service to perform,
His coat with dust of summer soiled,
His marrow chilled by wintry storm;
And now old age comes on apace,
But find of waning powers no trace.

This ancient, grizzled mule I sought,
If haply he'd be interviewed;
Since sure in Holy Wright 'tis taught,
How, where the barring angel stood,
A prophet, who was sure no saint,
Had listened to an ass's plaint.

Perhaps long residence on heights,
Where all know that the air is thin,
May have induced the airy flights
Of romance this mule reveled in,
Or mighty sweep of range and plain
Have gauged the workings of his brain.

But sure it is no poet's ear
E'er listened to a stranger tale;
The rocks re-echoed far and near,
The poet's face grew ashy pale,
As Balaam brayed sonorously,
His most astounding history.

He told of high-born ancestry,
Of noble sire and gentle dam,
Brothers and sisters, gay and free,
And his young life so bright and calm;
He traced a long, unbroken line
Of proud relations asinine.

Ambitions soon this scion seized
Which amply proved his pedigree;
He would go West, were parents pleased,
The Great Plains and the mountains see;
Nor should he e'er in quiet rest
Till he had climbed the Rocky's crest.

That he, this scheme which genius shows,
Found ways and means to carry out,
No one who mulish methods knows
Could ever have a lingering doubt.
It may suffice us now to say
That, like all mules, he had his way.

So now, his true vocation found,
He started on a proud career,
From plain to summit safe and sound
He carried hundreds every year —
Ladies who shrieked at steep ascent,
And many a scared but silent gent.

All this and more Old Balaam tells,
And feels his youth renewed thereby;
But now his bray in anger swells
And visciously his heels do fly,
While laboring to me to rehearse
His shameful wrongs in halting verse.

"I was a faithful mule," he said
"And meant to do the honest thing;
How was I shocked one night in bed,
To hear a sharp, resounding ring
That said, by click of telegraph,
My feed must be reduced one-half!

"The civil service, so it said,
  At last has got to be reformed,
  A start must somewhere soon be made,
  This citadel corrupt be stormed;
  But, since big guns might fire back
  They'd try at first a Pike's Peak jack.

"All this was too much to be borne;
  My plans with lightning speed were made,
  And I was free before the morn
  Escaped by strategy deep laid,
  And guided to the plains below,
  By the volcano's lurid glow.

"When I was down scarce half the way,
  Three mountain lions gave me chase,
  I met them: one yet lives they say,
  The rest in fragments sail through space!
  All who seen my backward reach
  Will know that solemn truth I teach.

"This victory gained, I came to where
  A stream of lava crossed the trail;
  The fiery current singed my hair,
  I labored, but without avail
  To cross the seething, boiling tide
  That must have beeen full ten yards wide.

"At last I spied a pine-crowned hill,
  O'er topping quiet the highest flame,
  Upon its crest I waited till
  A 'Colorado zephr' came,
  Then with my ample ears set sail,
  And over sped before the gale!

"So now I'm on my way to see
  The head men of the Narrow Gauge;
  If they'll but listen to my plea
  And these my burning wrongs assuage,
  Between us yet, I have no fears,
  We'll take the whole world by the ears.

"I'll ask them to extend their rail,
   Clear to the summit of the Peak,
   Run opposition to the trail,
   And all that Signal Service clique;
   'Old Prob' shall yet bewail the day
   When he put Balaam on half-pay.

"The Rio Grand runs, I hear,
   O'er cloud-wrapped summits, 'mid the snow,
   Clambers where mountain sheep might fear,
   Or winds through canyons far below,
   Success shall yet my efforts crown;
   Farewell, I'm off for Denver town!"

With heels and tail aloft in air,
   Old Balaam scampers o'er the plain,
   While lifts the poet's conscious hair
   And wildly throbs his swelling brain,
   At thoughts of what e'en mules may dare
   In this great country of light air!

From a pamphlet entitled *Colorado Springs-Manitou Springs*, "Compliments of the Business Men of Colorado Springs and Manitou Springs, Colorado," pp. 22-32.

THE SHOOTING OF THE CUP

By John G. Neihardt

This account of the famous incident which resulted in the shooting of Carpenter by Mike Fink during the enactment of an old frontier custom, is embodied by John G. Neihardt in one part of his long, epic reconstruction of plains history. Talbeau (or Talbott), the other one of the "three friends," tried to patch up the quarrel that had arisen over the love of an Indian maid.

They would have fought again,
   Had not the Major stepped between the men
   And talked the crisis by. And when 'twas past,
   Talbeau, intent to end the strife at last,
   Somehow persuaded Fink to make amends,

147

And, as a proof that henceforth they were friends,
Proposed the shooting of the whisky cup.
"Shure, b'y," said Mike, "we'll toss a copper up
And if 'tis heads I'll thry me cunning first.
As fer me joke, the tongue of me is cursed
Wid double j'ints — so let it be forgot!"
And so it was agreed.

                    They cleared a spot
And flipped a coin that tinkled as it fell.
A tiny sound — yet, like a midnight bell
That sets wild faces pressing at the pane,
Talbeau would often hear that coin again,
In vivid dreams, to waken terrified.
'Twas heads.

              And now the tall man stepped aside
And, beckoning Talbeau, he whispered: "Son,
If anything should happen, keep my gun
For old time's sake. And when the Major pays
In old St. Louis, drink to better days
When friends were friends, with what he's owing me."
Whereat the little man laughed merrily
And said: "Old Horse, you're off your feed today;
But if you've sworn an oath to blow your pay,
I guess the three of us can make it good!
Mike couldn't miss a target if he would."
"Well, maybe so," said Carpenter, and smiled.

A windless noon was brooding on the wild
And in the clearing, eager for the show,
The waiting trappers chatted. Now Talbeau
Stepped off the range. The tall man took his place,
The grin of some droll humor was on his face;
And when his friend was reaching for his head
To set the brimming cup thereon, he said:
"You won't forget I gave my gun to you
And all my blankets and my fixin's too?"
The small man laughed and, turning round, he cried:
"We're ready, Mike!"

A murmur ran and died
Along the double line of eager men.
Fink raised his gun, but set it down again
And blew a breath and said: "I'm gittin' dhry!
So howld yer noddle shtiddy, Bill, me b'y,
And don't ye shpill me whisky!" Cedar-straight
The tall man stood, the calm of brooding Fate
About him. Aye, and often to the end
Talbeau would see that vision of his friend —
A man-flower springing from the fresh green sod,
While, round about, the bushes burned with God
And mating peewees fluted in the brush.

They heard a gun lock clicking in the hush.
They saw Fink sighting — heard the rifle crack,
And saw beneath the spreading powder rack
The tall man pitching forward.

                                    Echoes fled
Like voices in a panic. Then Mike said:
"Bejasus, and ye've shpilled me whisky, Bill!"

A catbird screamed. The crowd stood very still
As though bewitched.

                    "And can't ye hear?" bawled Fink;
"I say, I'm dhry — and now ye've shpilled me drink!"
He stopped to blow the gasses from his gun.

And now men saw Talbeau. They saw him run
And stoop to peer upon the prostrate man
Where now the mingling blood and whisky ran
From oozing forehead and the tilted cup.
And in the hush a sobbing cry grew up:
"My God! You've killed him, Mike!"

                            Then growing loud,
A wind of horror blew among the crowd
And set it swirling round about the dead.
And over all there roared a voice that said:

149

"I niver mint to do it, b'ys, I swear!
The divil's in me gun!" Men turned to stare
Wild-eyed upon the center of that sound,
And saw Fink dash his rifle to the ground,
As 'twere the hated body of his wrong.

Once more arose that wailing, like a song,
Of one who called and called upon his friend.

John G. Neihardt, *The Song of Three Friends* (New York: The
Macmillan Co., 1919), pp. 83-87. Reprinted by special permission of
the author and of the publisher.

A TOUGH CUSS FROM BITTER CREEK

By James Barton Adams

That toughness was a "romantic pose" of the frontier is indicated
in this story, told by a shrewd, humorous newspaper versifier.
He'd take a human life as soon as he would take a drink,
His action with the ready gun was quicker than a wink,

He boasted of the many graves his vengeful hand had filled,
And of the bucketsful of blood he's humorously spilled.
Refuse to take a drink with him, and out would go your light,
Refrain from laughing at his jokes, and you would find a fight;
He was the vulture of the plains with whiskers on his beak,
This genuine, original tough cuss from Bitter Creek.

To Colorado state he drifted once upon a time
And struck a wondrous paying lead when Creede was in its prime,
And as the cash rolled in on him his toughness rolled away,
His tongue shed less profanity than in the early day.
He broke himself of killing men when hankering for fun,
A check-book filled the pocket which erstwhile concealed a gun,
And softness seemed to creep into the once case-hardened cheek
Worn by the original tough cuss from Bitter Creek.

Prompted by curiosity last Sabbath day I strolled
Into a leading Denver church, and there among the fold,
Dressed in a tony suit of black, up in the "Amen" row,
There sat a man I thought I'd seen back in the long ago.
His features wore a pious, calm, and sweet religious look,
His soft-toned eyes were glued upon an open prayer book,
And for a time I scarcely could believe that saint so meek
Was once the old original tough cuss from Bitter Creek.

James Barton Adams, *Breezy Western Verse* (Denver: Post Printing
and Publishing Co., 1899), p. 50.

TEXAS TYPES—"THE BAD MAN"

By *William Lawrence Chittenden*

The "bad man" of the unpoliced West often came, or boasted
that he had come, from Texas to plague other territories. This poem
takes this character at his own evaluation, but, soon after the closing
of the frontier, notes that the West could no longer afford to tolerate
such a predator, no matter how picturesque.

> He has a drooping winged moustache,
>   A little chin goatee;
> His face is hard, he dresses flash,
>   His eyes are strange to see.
>
> His boots have two-inch concave heels,
>   He wears a big slouch hat;
> He's full of *sand!* he never squeals,
>   Has too much nerve for that.
>
> Oh, yes, he gambles — *on the square* —
>   He sports gay diamond pins;
> He has that cool, dare-devil air
>   Whereby the gambler wins.
>
> You'll always find "he's killed his man"
>   Or "rounded up a band,"
> Or slain some greaser Mexican
>   Down on the Rio Grande.

151

And yet with all his scars and sin
    He seldom seeks a fight,
But when he does, he shoots to win
    Against all odds in sight.

You'll find him in the larger towns,
    He haunts the big bar-rooms,
And, ah! He haunts those silent mounds
    Which mark the city's tombs.

For like some flowers of colder climes,
    Which wither while yet green,
This Texas type of frosty times
    Soon leaves life's thorny scene.

For he is now beyond the age
    And order rules the day;
Texas has passed the pistol stage,
    The law has come to stay.

William Lawrence Chittenden, *Ranch Verses* (2nd edition, revised and enlarged; New York: G. P. Putnam's Sons, 1893), pp. 166-167.

THE LAY OF THE VIGILANTES

Anonymous

The American tradition of a self-appointed vigilance committee taking the law into its own hands in a lawless country controlled the worst excesses of frontier individualism but established some dangerous habit-precedents. This "swinging" ballad was included in John W. Cook's story of his father's, D. J. Cook's, career as a detective "in the Mountains and on the Plains."

By a local poet, on the hanging of a Georgetown, Colorado, criminal in 1872.

Not a bark was heard, not a warning note,
    As we o'er to the calaboose hurried;
Not a Thomas cat cleared his melodious throat
    Where our hero in slumber lay buried.

We entered his cell at the dead of night,
   The bolt with the jail keys turning,
The moon's pale crescent had sank out of sight,
   And never a lamp was burning.

No useless stogas encased his feet;
   And we saw, as we carefully bound him,
That he stood like a coward, dreading to meet
   The shades of the victims around him.

Few and short were the prayers he said —
   He did not have time to say long ones —
But he steadfastly gazed at the frame o'er his head
   And grieved that the posts were such strong ones.

We thought, as we hoisted him up from the ground
   And made the rope fast to a corner,
That the cool morning zephyrs would whisper around
   A corpse without ever a mourner.

Lightly they'll talk of the deed that is done,
   And wonder, "Who was it that hung him?"
Though little they'll grieve to see him hang on
   The beam where the "vigilance" swung him.

As soon as our cheerful task was done,
   Ere the light of the morning was firing
The peaks that glow in the rays of the sun,
   We prudently spoke of retiring.

Sternly and glady we looked on him there
   As we thought of his deeds dark and evil;
We heaved not a sigh and breathed not a prayer,
   But we left him alone with the Devil.

John W. Cook, *Hands Up* (Denver: The W. F. Robinson Printing Co., 1897), pp. 321-322.

THE RUIN OF BOBTAIL BEND

By James Barton Adams

The "Postcript Man" of the *Denver Evening and Sunday Post* wrote the epitaph, a half century ago, of the towns which were kept wide-open in order to profit from the pay-day sprees of cowboys and miners. His debt to Bret Harte is obvious.

In the early days in our own wild way we hurried the time along
In our Western style an' in manner I'll admit wasn't quite bong tong.
But the life we chose was our own, an' those who thought it was
    somewhat rude
Had the right to skate, fur to pull their freight to a moraler latitude.
Now I wish to say in emphatic way an' with honest intensity,
That we've seed the end of fun at the Bend, the fun that we used
    to see
Fur the moral wave that has come to save the camp from a sinful end
Has proved the ruin, the whole undoin' of pleasure at Bobtail Bend.

We could drink our booze in a way profuse an' buck at the faro games,
An' pound the floor till our hoofs was sore a swingin' the dance house
    dames,
An' we'd scrap an' fight to our hearts' delight with our other innocent
    sport,
With never a fear we would have to square ourselves in the jestice
    court.
If a man should scoot down the final chute that leads to the by an' by,
After leakin' his soul through a pistoled hole, there wasn't no hue an'
    cry,
But we'd plant him deep for eternal sleep in respectable sort o' way,
An' go on a spree to his memory an' forgit the thing in a day.

But the railroad come with the beatin' drum of the singin' Salvation
    gang,
An' the hills all 'round with the ruinous sound of encroachin' piety
    rang,
An' the eager throng that is drug along in the wake of the hoss of
    steam
Come a pourin' in to that nest o' sin in a rather unwelcome stream.
We was crowded back from the progress track in a damnably shameful
    way,

An' compelled to stand with the pistol hand unable to make a play,
An' the court o' law we with sorrow saw a backin' the moral game,
An' we dassent make a protestin' break through a wholesome fear o'
the same.

The cheery noise of the ol'-time boys was drowned by the church's bell,
The voice o' prayer riz up in the air, instead o' the whiskey yell,
An' we heerd the cries o' the school kids rise an' echo along the
stream,
An' the sportin' games and the hotfoot dames winked out as a pleasant
dream.
All the boys are gone, have meandered on, have scattered to other
parts,
On the ol' hillside lie a few that died, I reckon from broken hearts,
An' my race near run, I'm the only one that's left to await the end,
An' till Gabriel's horn I will sit an' mourn the ruin of Bobtail Bend.

James Barton Adams, *Breezy Western Verse* (Denver: The Post
Printing and Publishing Co., 1899), pp. 19-20.

CASEY'S TABLE D'HOTE

By Eugene Field

Field used the successful verse mannerisms of James Whitcomb
Riley and Bret Harte to celebrate the fine food served at the Miners'
Hotel in Gold Hill, an old mining camp in Boulder County, Colorado.
He took poetic license with "the year '63," as he did with the name
"Red Hoss Mountain," for the thirty-room log hostel was built in
1872 by Charles Wentworth. It still contains many of its original
furnishings and is run as a tourist resort.

Oh, them days on Red Hoss Mountain, when the skies was fair 'nd
blue;
When the money flowed like likker, 'nd the folks was brave 'nd true!
When the nights wuz crisp 'nd balmy, 'nd the camp wuz all astir,
With the joints all throwed wide open 'nd no sheriff to demur!
Oh, them times on Red Hoss Mountain in the Rockies fur away —
There's no sich place nor times like them as I kin find to-day!

What though the camp hez busted? I seem to see it still
A-lyin', like it love it, on that big 'nd warty hill;
And I feel a sort of yearnin' 'nd a chokin' in my throat
When I think of Red Hoss Mountain 'nd of Casey's tabble dote!

Well, yes; it's true I struck it rich, but that don't cut a show
When one is old 'nd feeble 'nd it's nigh his time to go;
The money that he's got in bonds or carries to invest
Don't figger with a codger who has lived a life out West;
Us old chaps like to set around, away from folks 'nd noise,
'Nd think about the sights we seen and things we done when boys;
The which is why I love to set 'nd think of them old days
When all us Western fellers got the Colorado craze, —
And that is why I love to set around all day 'nd gloat
On thoughts of Red Hoss Mountain 'nd of Casey's tabble dote.

This Casey wuz an Irishman — you'd know it by his name
And by the facial features appertainin' to the same,
He'd lived in many places 'nd had done a thousand things,
From the noble art of actin' to the work of dealin' kings,
But, somehow, hadn't caught on; so, driftin' with the rest,
He drifted for a fortune to the undeveloped West,
And he come to Red Hoss Mountain when the little camp wuz new,
When the money flowed like likker, 'nd the folks wuz brave 'nd true;
And, havin' been a stewart on a Mississippi boat,
He opened up a caffy 'nd he run a tabble dote.

The bar wuz long 'nd rangey, with a mirrer on the shelf,
'Nd a pistol, so that Casey, when required, could help himself;
Down underneath there wuz a row of bottled beer 'nd wine,
'Nd a keg of Burbun whiskey of the run of '59;
Upon the walls wuz pictures of hosses 'nd of girls, —
Not much on dress, perhaps, but strong on records 'nd on curls!
The which had been identified with Casey in the past, —
The hosses and the girls, I mean, — and both wuz mighty fast!
But all these fine attractions wuz of precious little note
By the side of what wuz offered at Casey's tabble dote.

There wuz half-a-dozen tables altogether in the place,
And the tax you had to pay upon vitals wuz a case;
The boardin'-houses in the camp protested 'twuz a shame
To patronize a robber, which this Casey wuz the same!
They said a case was robbery to tax for ary meal;
But Casey tended strictly to his biz, 'nd let 'em squeal;
And presently the boardin'-houses all began to bust,
While Casey kept on sawin' wood 'nd layin' in the dust;
And oncet a trav'lin' editor from Denver City wrote
A piece back to his paper, puffin' Casey's tabble dote.

A tabble dote is different from orderin' aller cart:
In one case you git all there is, in t'other, only part!
And Casey's tabble dote began in French — as all begin, —
And Casey's ended with the same, which is to say, with "vin";
But in between wuz every kind of reptile, bird, 'nd beast,
The same like you can git in high-toned restauraws down east;
'Nd windin' up wuz cake or pie, with coffee demy tass,
Or, sometimes, floatin' Ireland in a soothin' kind of sass
That left a sort of pleasant ticklin' in a feller's throat,
'Nd made him hanker after more of Casey's tabble dote.

The very recollection of them puddin's 'nd them pies
Brings a yearnin' to my buzzum 'nd the water to my eyes;
'Nd seems like cookin' nowadays aint what it used to be
In camp in Red Hoss Mountain in that year of '63;
But, maybe, it is better, 'nd, maybe, I'm to blame —
I'd like to be a livin' in the mountains jest the same —
I'd like to live that life again when skies wuz fair 'nd blue,
When things wuz run wide open 'nd men wuz brave 'nd true;
When brawny arms the flinty ribs of Red Hoss Mountain smote
For wherewithal to pay the price of Casey's tabble dote.

And you, O cherished brother, a-sleepin' way out west;
With Red Hoss Mountain huggin' you close to its lovin' breast, —
Oh, do you dream in your last sleep of how we use to do,
Of how we worked our little claims together, me 'nd you?
Why, when I saw you last a smile wuz restin' on your face,
Like you wuz glad to sleep forever in that lonely place;

And so you wuz, 'nd I'd be, too, if I wuz sleepin' so.
But, bein' how a brother's love aint for the world to know,
Whenever I've this heartache 'nd this chokin' in my throat,
I lay it all to thinkin' of Casey's tabble dote.

Eugene Field, *A Little Book of Western Verse* (New York: Charles
Scribner's Sons, 1889), pp. 1-7.

OLD RED HOSS MOUNTAIN

By Cy Warman

Mining towns are monuments to pioneering effort — or to human
frustration, as you please. Warman accepted the supposition that
Eugene Field's Red Hoss Mountain was in the Gold Hill Mining
District, which was created March 7, 1859. At one time 2,000 persons
swarmed in the little camp called Gold Hill, up Boulder Canyon.

I've been to Red Hoss Mountain, where Field once dwelt and wrote;
I've seen the Place de Casey, but Casey's table d'hote
Is gone; and so is Casey. A solitary pine
The fires have spared now shadows the Gosh-all-Hemlock Mine.

There's not a cabin standing, so that a man can say,
"The conversazzhyony in this abode held sway."
Aye, everything has perished save earth and sky and space;
The bard of Red Hoss Mountain is gone to his own place.

The mines are all abandoned, the rain-washed trails are dim;
But where are all the people who tramped these trails with him?
And where are all the actors he staged here long ago,
When magpies, "like winged shadows, were fluttering to and fro"?

The trees that made the forest have fallen, one by one,
Until Old Red Hoss Mountain lies bare beneath the sun;
Yet, in the deathlike stillness that hangs upon the air,
I love to sit and fancy I feel his presence there.
Sweet soul! He knew a heartache if e'en a robin cried,
Then how he must have sorrowed when Martha's baby died;

When strong, rough men stood weeping who had not wept for years;
With Martha's heart nigh breaking and Sorry Tom in tears.

. . . . . .

The brook that sang so "lonesome-like, an' loitered on its way"
Is singing just as softly and lonesome-like to-day.
One pine above the hemlock and just one willow weeps
Down in the ragged canyon where "Martha's younket" sleeps.

Cy Warman, *Songs of Cy Warman* (Boston: Rand Avery Co.; Toronto:
McLeod & Allen, 1911), pp. 48-49.

HOW WE BUILT A CHURCH AT ASHCROFT

By Jack Leahy

The Irish were in the midst of the fights, frolics, and work
which built the West. This account of the building of a Roman
Catholic Church at the small mining camp above Aspen, Colorado,
was written down by Ashcroft's mayor, hermit, and last survivor. He
claimed to be an oral bard, in the Celtic tradition, but he wrote
down the following narrative around 1880. It circulated in manuscript
for many years before it appeared in print.

Come all ye Irish gentlemen, a story I would tell
Of St. Tim's Church at Ashcroft, and all that there befell.
Since snows did fall and streams run down from lofty Castle Peak,
More witching spot could ne'er be found, of poet man to speak;
Or lovely vales, bestrewn with flowers, or columbine more rare;
Or sparkling waters foaming down, or azure skies more fair.

    The faithful met at Paddy's with chairman Deacon Perch;
    Six trustees were elected and empowered to build a church.
    The reason why—the camp was shocked one evening's stage to
        meet,
    A portly dame, one Madame Nobbs with six from Holliday Street.
    We all were high protectionists, or, as the case may be,
    The vote stood ninety-nine to one 'gainst reciprocity.

The trustees all were moral men with here and there a flaw;
Brilliant Lawyer Callahan, with perpetual motion jaw;
And Jim McCool of Provo, of whom gossip doth aver
That he was one of the elect at the Meadow Massacre;
And roaring Mike, sleek Broker Shark and bibulous Deacon Perch,
With Billy Shale the expert, were the trustees of the church.

 A site was soon selected on a knoll on Silver Hill
 That overlooked the valley and the Rocky Mountain Mill.
 The hearts of all beholders, filled with solemn, holy love,
 A flame divine reminding them of their prospects far above,
 Forgot their prospects in the hills and all their earthly woes,
 With expert, side and apex rights, and gun plays with their foes.

They dispensed with all formalities, they were business to the brim,
With but one thought to dedicate, to the Irish saint, St. Tim.
The announcement brought forth hearty praise from many fervent
 hearts,
Who knew the Saint first introduced our silver in the arts,
And spread its use as money, and in every way had he
Fostered and protected it, a benignant tutelary.

 And Irish hearts were light that day, they rambled through the
  town
 And drank and cussed and fought and prayed and danced to Garry
  Owen.
 In all their past adversity, since they were forced to roam,
 To leave the Isle of memory dear, and wander far from home,
 This was the first occasion, when in all the interim,
 Such honor had been done to him, their patron saint, St. Tim.

The Reverend Father Placid next day arrived in camp
From o'er the range at Canyon, a most scintillant lamp,
That ne'er beneath the bushel hid, but in refulgent rays
Caused adamantine hearts to break, reluctant tongues to praise
The glory of our Heavenly King, and her we hold as Queen,
And acknowledge with contrition the lowly Nazarene.

 The trustees met the Father, led by Honorable Callahan,
 Who knew the small law or equity and practiced catch as catch
  can.

They were ushered to the presence of this calm and holy man,
And without an introduction the lawyer thus began:
"With apostolic benediction, your assistance we implore,
And Jehovah will reward you when you reach the golden shore.

"We bespeak your riper wisdom, and pray you us advise
In this spiritual proceeding, this heavenly enterprise,
In which we lay our treasures, in haec, ad hoc, quoddam,
At his feet and beg his favor for our sacrificial lamb,
To-wit, the lofty spire we very soon shall raise
On Silver Hill above the vale, where Ashcroft lies in tranquil ways.

A silence spread for yet awhile, then up rose Broker Shark;
"Most reverend Sir, we hold that this shall ever be a mark
Of holy veneration, such grace doth Heaven lend
To fulfillment of the law, 'Be thou faithful to the end.'
Five thousand plunks are promised us and now are fully due,
With two thousand for a parsonage, on Hold-Up Avenue."

Father Placid rose in rapture and shook each trustee's hand,
"Behold in me a servant who obeys divine command.
To do the will of Him on high, before you I appear,
To glorify His holy name out on this wild frontier,
Where I find three bustling hamlets, or cities so to speak,
Nestling in this quiet valley near the shade of Castle Peak.

"With Hunley's in the center and Kellogg lying south,
And Ashcroft joining on the north, I find that Pine Creek's mouth
Is centrally located, between the sister towns;
Then built the church on one of those majestic rising mounds
And throw the life-line out—." "Cut her short," yelled Roaring
    Mike;
"You're prospectin' a blind lead, in a big slumgullion dike.

"I tell you, boys, I've tried to be a sober Christian man
Since I let the light-o-day shine through Apache Dan.
Deak Perch knows well that Hunley duck on me did get the draw,
And but for good old Calico Sal this day I'd never saw.
If the church is built at Hunley's I stand right here to tell,
That fifty churches in a row wouldn't keep 'em out of Hell."

Quoth Jim McCool: "That latest pill has a most bitter taste,
But, brethren, in such matters we should never act in haste.
As for my sins, I will admit the bunch I ran last year
Were bred betwixt a brandin' iron and a festive Texas steer.
'Tis said I am not married, but Parson—well, of course
I cannot marrry her by law, 'till she gets her divorce.

"To save my immortal soul from Hell, with all my will and power
I've entered in the vineyard at this eleventh hour,
To be a Christian soldier, by my colors standing true,
To do that unto others just what I wish to do.
If the church is built at Hunley's I have but one desire:
To visit it in broad daylight and set the shack on fire."

Then Deacon Perch arose, saying: "We must this day decide.
As Broker Sharp has option, down to Devanny's slide.
To me it feels like pulling teeth to be giving up the knoll,
But I'll do even more than that to save my immortal soul.
Where'er it's built, you'll find me there with God's praise upon
my tongue;
Thank God, I'm glad to take my drink from the spigot or the
bung."

Then forth stood Billy Shale, who'd been silent until now,
With perspiration steaming from his scientific brow.
"Your conclusions, worthy father, the very gods do mock,
Our Savior bid St. Peter build his church upon a rock.
By blow-pipe test we find the knoll hard, massive diorite;
On the west eruptive granite, on the east flint dolomite.

"Earthquake and volcano-proof forever 'twill remain;
It hits the northwest corner of the Rock of Ages vein.
Theology and geology go ever hand in hand;
If the church is built at Pine Creek you build it on the sand.
The mound is mere deposit of a glacial moraine,
And if you put it at that spot your building is in vain."

Father Placid then got ruffled and lost his peaceful smile;
"You may build your church at Hunley's, at Kellogg or a mile
This side of nowhere, as you please. I'm well content that when

You get your just reward on earth, I'll see you in the pen;
My duties there I will resume and greet you when you come;
Your hearts are hard as Silver Hill, to the voice of God you're dumb."

Next morn the Father left, with dissension in the flock.
Some shouted, "Put her on the sand," some, "Stick her on the rock."
To pristine resolution, though, the trustees all were game,
On Silver Hill they blasted and erected high the frame;
But funds that were forthcoming are yet forthcoming still,
And nothing more was ever done at St. Tim's on the hill.

Her Nobbs, the Madame, no less bold than she of scarlet fame,
Between two suns went up the hill and stole away the frame,
And builded her a house upon the sands of Castle Creek,
As if to mock the teachings of our Saviour, mild and meek.
"God is not mocked." Ye sinners, hear and heed the fearful fate
Of Nobbs' gay crowd, and mend your ways before it is too late.

Cathedral Dome tossed off a slide where slide was never known,
That with increasing fury ran from e'en its topmost comb;
And gathering boulders as it ran, down through the Pine Creek slope,
With vengeance from on high leaped down, and buried without hope
Of rescue, all that mocking crowd of light and erring folk,
Who thought on failure of our church to perpetrate a joke.

From *Rocky Mountain Life,* vol. 2, no. 7 (Denver: September, 1947), pp. 30-31.

THE LODGE ROOM OVER SIMPKINS' STORE

By Lawrence N. Greenleaf

Fraternal organizations, as well as churches, helped to solidify frontier society. Freemasonry had as laureate Colorado's first published poet, who spent the latter part of the 19th century gracing public occasions with his effusions. He was Past Grand Master of Colorado.

The plainest lodge room in the land was over Simpkins' store,
Where Friendship Lodge had met each month for fifty years or more.
When o'er the earth the moon, full-orbed, had cast her brightest beams,
The brethren came from miles around on horseback and in teams.
And O! what hearty grasp of hand, what welcome met them there,
As mingling with the waiting groups they slowly mount the stair,
Exchanging fragmentary news or prophesies of crop,
Until they reach the Tyler's room and current topics drop,
To turn their thoughts to nobler themes they cherish and adore,
And which were heard on meeting night up over Simpkins' store.

To city eyes, a cheerless room, long usage had defaced,
The tell-tale lines of lath and beam on wall and ceiling traced.
The light from oil-fed lamps was dim and yellow in its hue,
The carpet once could pattern boast, though now 'twas lost to view.
The altar and the pedestals that marked the stations three,
The gate-post pillars topped with balls, the rude-carved letter "G,"
Were village joiner's clumsy work, with many things beside,
Where beauty's lines were all effaced and ornament denied.
There could be left no lingering doubt, if doubt there was before,
The plainest lodge room in the land was over Simpkins' store.

While musing thus on outward form the meeting time drew near,
And we had glimpse of inner life through watchful eye and ear.
When Lodge convened at gavel's sound with officers in place,
We looked for strange, conglomerate work, but could no errors trace.
The more we saw, the more we heard, the greater our amaze,
To find those country brethren there so skilled in Masons' ways.
But greater marvels were to come before the night was through,
Where unity was not mere name, but fell on heart like dew.
Where tenets had the mind imbued, and truths rich fruitage bore,
In plainest Lodge room in the land, up over Simpkins' store.

To hear the record of their acts was music to the ear,
We sing of deeds unwritten which on angel's scroll appear.
A WIDOW'S CASE—FOUR HELPLESS ONES—Lodge funds were
    running low,
A dozen brethren sprang to feet and offers were not slow.
Food, raiment, things of needful sort, while one gave load of wood,
Another, shoes for little ones, for each gave what he could.

Then spake the last: "I haven't things like these to give—but then,
Some ready money may help out"—and he laid down a TEN.
Were brother cast on darkest square upon life's checkered floor,
A beacon light to reach the white—was over Simpkins' store.

Like scoffer who remained to pray, impressed by sight and sound,
The faded carpet 'neath our feet was now like holy ground.
The walls that had such dingy look were turned celestial blue,
The ceiling changed to canopy where stars were shining through.
Bright tongues of flame from altar leaped, the G was vivid blaze,
All common things seemed glorified by heaven's reflected rays.
O! wondrous transformation wrought through ministry of love—
Behold the LODGE ROOM BEAUTIFUL!—fair type of that above,
The vision fades—the lesson lives! and taught as ne'er before,
In plainest Lodge room in the land—up over Simpkins' store.

Reprinted from a broadside urging subscription to the *Rocky Mountain Mason*, dated November 19, 1898.

THE FIGHT AT NEVADAVILLE

Anonymous

In the old mining towns such as Nevadaville and Russell Gulch, adjoining Central City, Colorado, when Cornish Cousin Jack and Yankee Cousin Bill mixed in celebration, you could look for the roof to come off.

Nevadaville upon a hill,
    The home of Cousin Jack and Jill,
Was once a hustling town, they say,
    With lots of work and lots of pay;
But now she's dead, as dead as—well,
    She's just the Ante-room of hell.

Last Friday night they had a dance
    At which the town went in a trance,
As with the eyes of wild dement
    They saw the Red's entertainment—
Spiced with the gems of speech divine
    And specter charm of pantomime.

Then in the midst of all the joy
King Barley captured one poor boy,
And with his fingers bent up double
He forthwith sought a little trouble;
Which same he found, and in a tussle
Got mixed up with a lad from Russell.

The boys from Russell were not slow,
They went right out into the snow—
Pulled off their coats and then with ease
Proceeded to roll up their sleeves,
And with the science of a hen
The whole darn bunch just waded in.

When all these fistic fights were fought,
They all went down where booze was bought,
And there they camped 'til whistles blew
(And some a little later too),
While promises were made by all
To come enmasse to our next ball.

From a manuscript copy secured by Caroline Bancroft of Denver, on September 27, 1942, from Mrs. (Jack) Gertrude Riedl, Russell Gulch, Colorado.

GRAND OPENING OF THE PEOPLE'S THEATRE

By O. J. Goldrick

From the *Denver Daily Evening News*, December 2, 1861, page 3, columns 2 and 3: "Messrs. Langrishe and Dougherty opened their new and elegant dramatic institution on Saturday night, to an audience, which, for the style, intelligence and respectability, could not easily be eclipsed elsewhere throughout the border states and settlements. Had the building been of double dimensions, it doubt less would have been still filled to its increased capacity, on this occasion, as crowds went away, being unable to gain admission, and crowds who wanted to be there, remained at home being aware of the jam that would be encountered. The 'Mistletoe Bough' was put upon the stage in a manner which could not well be excelled in

166

most of the old established theatres, and the afterpiece of 'My Neighbor's Wife' was presented with a freshness that smacked of something
new . . . . Below we give the opening address, written and recited
by Mr. O. J. Goldrick, of this office."

Pike's Peakers! All! From whatsoever climes,
You've "crossed the Plains," to see or search the mines,
We greet you! here tonight!
And bid you welcome to the sight,
And sound of what may on this People's stage be done—
To present Virtue bright, or cause you Vice to shun,—
To show up Nature's traits,—"shoot folly as it flies,"
And "catch the manners, living, as they rise!"
From Shakespeare's genius, and Ben Jonson's powers,
To grow and gladden, like the mead with showers,
As their high strains of inspiration roll,
Cheer up the heart, and elevate the soul,
And to your heart, and soul, and ear, and eye,
Teach beauty, truth and love, and melody.

At every epoch on the world's page,
Civilization has been aided by the stage,
From Sophocles of old, who in the isles of Greece
First produced plays with but a single piece,
From Caesar's time, beneath St. Peter's dome,
When Roscius was the actor for Imperial Rome,
Down through the changes of the Saxon line,
The Drama's aim was always to refine;
"A friend to Freedom and the virtuous cause,
A foe to tyrants and to unjust laws."

Now, who can tell, if, as the poets say,
"Westward the star of Empire takes its way,"
But e'er some dozen moons shall wax and wane,
Our "Peoples" here shall prove a "Drury Lane,"
Where "stars" from London, Paris, New York, and elsewhere,
May mount the "iron horse" and play a season here!
Behold what progress, and what change sublime,
Has here occurred within scarce three years' time,
Upon this brow of old St. Charles town,

Where late the Arapahoe and Cheyenne did frown
On "pale-faced" pilgrims who came here to seek,
For shining chunks of gold in Cherry Creek,
Ere yet the Kansas boys had "jumped" Old Nichol's claim,
"Jayhawked" the "Saint" and "wrung in" Denver's name,
Now stands this temple—this Dramatic Hall,
A monument of taste—a source of pride to all,
Where Langrishe—the lion of dramatic war,
And Mike," the miner of Grass Valley Bar,
Have shown the works and enterprising zeal,
What two can do united, shoulder to the wheel.

We greet you here to-night, on Colorado's plain,
From every section of our vast domain.
Here, where, as yet, we stand alone on squatter's rights,
But stand, as yet, thank God, beneath the stars and stripes!
Here on this highway between the East and West,
'Neath peaks and mountains, from whose snowy crest,
The air of freedom, like grace of God,
Falls on the citizens, and fructifies our sod,
Dispels Disunion and its impious band,
From off this backbone of Columbia's land,
Here where our Gilpin, many years gone by,
Foretold our future, with a prophet's eye,
And where young Fremont—the pathfinder bold,
With patriotism buoyant, and bravery yet untold,
Paved out the way for pioneers—for nations yet to come—
Where, through God's aid, shall ever wave the flag of Washington!

From *The Rocky Mountain News,* December 2, 1861.

CARRIER'S ADDRESS
January 1, 1862

Anonymous

Until well into the twentieth century, American newspapers prepared verse reviews of the preceding year, to be sold or presented for a gratuity by their carriers on New Year's Day. In the growing West, these New Year addresses are important records of how contemporaries felt about our past history. Most of the local references are still clear enough, as are the national events referred to in the following.

Dear Friends and Patrons of the DENVER NEWS!
On South Platte's Plains or 'mid the Mountain dews,
In thriving towns throughout our golden mines,
Please pause awhile, and read your Carrier's lines;
And should his carol be but poorly sung,
His muse's a novice, and the country's young!

Since New Year's last, Columbia's sacred Star
Has been bedimmed by bloody civil war;
The Union heart has beat with travail throes,
The Union ship has sailed 'midst myriad foes;
But yet, thank God! her course is onward, on;
Her harbor piers stand firm at Washington.

Although, at first, Fort Sumter has been won
From old Kentucky's gallant Anderson,
And our brave boys, in panic, beat retreat,
For lack of numbers, at Bull's Run defeat,
Our Nation's Eagle, with proud wing and free,
Still soars o'er White House and from sea to sea!

And ere another circling year shall dawn
Upon this country, this broad, Freedom's lawn,—
With Scott's precedents and McClellan's skill—
We trust our troops will dark Secession kill,
Restore our empire, through from lake to sea,
The pride of earth, the haven of the Free!

169

The twelve month past, so fraught with trouble East,
Has wrought grave change 'mid us folks here far West.
"Pike's Peak" no more retains its wonted fame,
For all things now bear Colorado's name.
In place of "Bummer" and of "Vigy" rule,
We're governed now, like lads at Charter School.

Instead of Steele, and "Providential" brawl,
Now Gilpin edicts, and the sage Judge Hall
Deals out the "dictas" by which all are held
As strictly straight as soldiers at Camp Weld.
(While on parade, we mean, and not abroad,
When they, through thirst, are forced to "run the guard.")

And, though some folks who hold the "inside track,"
Incline to doubt these rulers will come back,
Their regal reins are well and ably held,
At least thus far, by Lewis Ledyard Weld,
Our fourth chief ruler, now, in point of fact,
Through Grace of God and the Organic Act.

Instead of gold dust and the coin in hand,
Pass current now "brass filings and black sand."
Like Gregory leads with countless tunnel shafts,
We've all been "bored," with Gilpin's countless "drafts,"—
Drawn on the U. S., without "days of grace,"
Which "ain't quite right," says Secretary Chase.

How changed the scene, thro' Denver city wards,
Since the "Platte Rangers" and the "Ragged Guards,"
With rations scant and regimentals old,
Traversed the "town-site" and by night patrolled,
To guard our shanties, 'mid first winter's snows.
From wolves and Indians, and, worse, pale-faced foes!

Those wolves are "strychnined," and those red men roam
Arkansas' bottoms, their old winter home.
The town's now "finished," since thro' safety fears,

We've quartered here a thousand Volunteers,
With Captains gallant and a Colonel brave,
To whip the Texans and this country save!

Our First Assembly and th' Election o'er,
Pass'd off triumphant, Union to the core;
Its mighty voice spoke out both strong and stern,
For Printer, through to Constable, short term.
Our Members, many, did sound wisdom show,
Save, perhaps, one, who always voted "No!"

In home affairs, as well as those abroad,
We've reasons many to feel justly proud.
Our lines have fallen in auspicious place,
On lands just surveyed now, by General Case.
Our public wants, if right and just it stands,
Will meet success, in H. P. Bennet's hands.

Friends, Miners, Merchants, Artists, Farmers too!
We wish you luck thro' Eighteen Sixty Two!
May all your "plates" with rich "amalgam" fill,
And hogs be fat, that next New Year's ye kill.
From Denver, Gregory, thro' to Buckskin Joe,
May all amass what "makes th' mare to go!"

And ye, fair ladies, Colorado o'er,
Whose pleasing presence, like rich "dust" in store,
Dispels our wants, our cup of comfort fills,—
We wish you, all, the best that Heaven wills,
Maidens, girls, wives, and widows too,—
Who'd be a Carrier but for meeting you?

But to be brief, and lest our friend should think
That we've lost sight of the main point—your "chink,"
We'll close our rhyme—our reputation save,
And kindly thank you for whate'er you give;
The more the better,—as it tells and pays,
Like bread on waters—after many days!

From *The Rocky Mountain News,* Denver, Colorado, January 1, 1862.

171

THE CAMELS HAVE COME

Anonymous

This song may remind us of the United States government's attempt to use camels as draught animals in the Great American Desert, but its immediate occasion was a newspaper hoax. On March 31. 1866, the *Rocky Mountain News* announced that during the night there would arrive in Denver a camel train belonging to Don Raphael Grandjean, plantation owner of the Rio Hondo, New Mexico. "This train," said the *News*, "consists in part of six full grown camels, which the gentleman is bringing in here loaded with wool."

On April 2, the paper printed the following item: "By some unaccountable error those camels got upon the wrong road and went to Golden City, where they will be loaded and return to New Mexico, without visiting Denver until the *First of April,* 1867. It was a source of great disappointment to many, who visited the Elephant Corral yesterday to see them." Three nights later, patrons of the Denver Theatre were entertained with the following song, sung by Captain Andres to the tune "The Campbells Are Coming."

> "The Camels are coming," huzza, huzza!
> Let the news go abroad to all, near and far;
> Oh, take a long breath and start on the run
> At the Elephant Corral the camels have come.
> They've such great humps on their backs and, so lean.
> Ask Cheney, for he has been there and seen;
> But don't be alarmed, they're harmless, 'tis true,
> Go early, go quick, and get a good view.
>
> CHORUS—The Camels are coming, etc.
>
> "Oh, the Camels are coming!" Oh such was the cry,
> On the first day of April, if the papers don't lie,
> And to see the grand sight the people did go,
> By two's and by four's like old Noah's show.
> Jim Cavanaugh threw his law books in a pile,
> And rushed from his office in true lawyer style,
> Being bent upon seeing the camels so near,
> But when he came back, he was saying, "Oh dear!"

CHORUS—The Camels are coming, etc.

"The Camels are coming." I thought so myself,
And was scratching about to gather the pelf,
For caging the birds, and showing them 'round,
At a dollar a head, to the people in town.
The man with his bears and I did agree,
To double his show and go snacks with me,
To make a small stake and show off our mit,
But instead of our fun 'twas ourselves that got bit.

CHORUS—The Camels are coming, etc.

The people that wont, —their names I could tell,
But they all seem shy because 'twas a sell,
The Camels came in without any delay,
And all got fooled on All Fool's day.
In the NEWS it was published—not just a jest.
Some blame Doc. Wharton, and some Capt. West;
The thing was well done, the folks to amuse.
So, if you got sold,—Charge it all to the NEWS.

CHORUS—The Camels are coming, etc.

From *The Rocky Mountain News*, April 6, 1866.

DOING RAILROADS FOR *THE ROCKY MOUNTAIN NEWS*

By Cy Warman

Denver, which had five daily newspapers at one time, is, like Chicago, a city of journalistic legend about the "wild, free old days." The papers were often sparsely staffed. This humorous exaggeration about the first and longest-lasting of them is a rich local color story.

It was sometime in the P.M. of the fall of '92
I had cashed in the Creede Chronicle—had nothing much to do—
I had seen the man of leisure who was loafing on the street,
Who had every fad and fashion from his head down to his feet,

And this prince was a reporter; so I shined my Sunday shoes,
And went down to do the railroads for *The Rocky Mountain News*.

Now the city man was Martin, from McCullagh's *Democrat*,
And he glanced over his glasses as I doffed my derby hat—
I had owned a daily paper in the springtime of the year,
That had sunk ten thousand dollars; I had nothing then to fear—
I had planned that in the morning I would dally with the muse,
In the P.M. do the railroad for *The Rocky Mountain News*.

"Well, ahem, ahem!" said Martin, clearing cobwebs from his throat,
While the smoke from his Havana round my face began to float;
"I presume that you're in touch with the officials here in town,
Having worked for them; however, I shall have to send you down
To the police court." Then he coughed again and shed his overshoes,
"That's included with the railroads on *The Rocky Mountain News*."

I assured him that the railroads to my mind would be a snap,
I could talk about train orders, and could write a lead and lap;
I could banquet with the president, or if I chose could take
A turn down in the freight yards, 'mong the men who twist the brake;
I could hobnob with the fireman while he augured out his flues—
I could surely do the railroads for *The Rocky Mountain News*.

"We're a little bit short-handed—you will do the county courts;
And this evening, after dinner, drift around among the sports;
There's a prizefight down at Murphy's." Then he paused and rubbed
        his head.
"That's all I have to say now," this encyclopedia said.
I didn't say a word then, but I thought it beat the Jews
The way they did the railroads down on *The Rocky Mountain News*.

I had buttoned up my overcoat, was headed for the stair,
When the quidnunc's restless fingers wandered thru his wealth of hair;
I had reached the elevator when he called me back and said:
"You will have to do the statehouse, for the statehouse man is dead."
My poor heart sank within me, but I couldn't well refuse,
Since it all went with the railroads on *The Rocky Mountain News*.

"See the concerts at the churches in the early eve," he said;
"Try and do Dean Hart's cathedral where an heiress is to wed
An English dude from Dublin—Freeman won't be here today.
You may write about a column on What Old-Timers Say
About the San Juan Gold Excitement—but mind, we can't excuse
Any neglect of the railroads on *The Rocky Mountain News.*"

I was off. For ten long hours thru the slush and snow and sleet,
Up the stone steps of the statehouse, out again and down the street,
Till I paused to feed at midnight—hit the bottle till my soup
Seemed a sea of strange assignments—every oyster was a scoop,
Mused on how the other papers would be burdened with the blues,
When they read about the railroads in *The Rocky Mountain News.*

After lunch I read my copy, which told how the Rio Grande
Had a good house, and the organ was wide open working sand.
'Twas a cold day for the criminals who proceed in wicked ways,
For they raided all the churches, and the dean got twenty days,
The soprano dropped her crown, the policeman warped his flues,
"Throwing in too much cold water," said *The Rocky Mountain News.*

Big strike on the reservation, all the Navajos went out,
How the toughs had met at Trinity to hear the second shout,
All the preachers in their pulpits piling up their little piles
On Jim Corbett. How the ladies down at Murphy's blocked the aisles.

*   *   *

The next day I got a letter that would give a man the blues:
"This is good, but we can't read it," Signed: *"The Rocky Mountain
    News."*

Now I view the proud reporter as he swiftly sallies by.
A bob-tailed flush upon his cheek, a twinkle in his eye;
He has my sincere sympathy—I do not want his place,
I pine not for his twinkle, nor the flush upon his face;
No matter what inducements, I invariably refuse,
Since the day I did the railroads for *The Rocky Mountain News.*

Reprinted in *The Rocky Mountain News,* 75th Anniversary Edition,
April 22, 1934.

THE CURTAIN
(Old Tabor Grand Opera House)
By Jean Milne Gower

Some years ago the Tabor Grand Opera House, built in 1881 in Denver by Senator H. A. W. Tabor at a cost of $1,000,000, was converted into a motion picture house and its interior greatly altered. But its old curtain, bearing a painting of a Roman city in ruins and Kingsley's lines, quoted below, still remains and is occasionally lowered.

> "So fleet the works of men, back to the earth again;
>   Ancient and holy things fade like a dream."
> These, Kingsley's words, remain like a beloved refrain
>   Blending the things that are with things that seem.
> Once more the curtain falls, and crumbled like cloistered walls,
>   The mirrored columns float in the lagoon;
> Ghosts of dream-laden days pass by as in a maze,
>   Wistfully, silently—vanished too soon.

Jean Milne Gower, *The Kaleidoscope, Little Pictures of Colorado* (Denver: The Miles & Dryer Printing Co., 1923), p. 49.

THE WOMAN IN THE WAGON
By Clyde Robertson

The boastful and heroic mood of the gold and cattle frontier is replaced by an emphasis upon hardship and disillusionment in the literature of the homesteaders. This poem of rural realism, in the tradition of Edwin Markham's *The Man with the Hoe,* was chosen as the J. Roberts Foster 1925 international prize ballad by the *Poetry Review* of London.

> She stares from out the wagon as
> It trails the dimming road,
> A huddled unkempt being bowed
> Beneath life's driving goad.
>
> On, on through torrid summer days,
> And chill and waning year,

On, on through miles of trackless waste,
Where grinning white skulls leer.

The never-ending grind of days
And nights—the dusk—the dawn—
A checkerboard of tortures where
She moves, a helpless pawn.

She stares from out the wagon as
She dreams of other days—
A youth and a maid—a shaded path
Where fragrant hawthorn sways.

Her little hand, so soft, he kissed
And smoothed her curls so fair—
She twists with fumbling fingers now
The wisp of tangled hair.

Back home! back home! her haunted eyes
Have long since ceased to weep,
She only stares and huddles now
A broken, unkempt heap.

The lure of unknown lands had called
To him, her lover bold;
Beyond the hills and plains there lay
A country steeped in gold.

The spirit of adventure thrilled!
His man heart all forgot
The promises he made to her
Who vowed to share his lot.

The little home beside the hedge
Where hawthorne grew bereft;
Lone canvas covered wanderings
Were all she now had left.

Lone wanderings and memories—
She was no soldier brave

In search of wild adventurings
And desert lands to save!

She was a woman who had dreamed
Of children and a home;
It lay, her child, on bleaching plain
Beneath a pile of stone.

On, on the wagon creeps apace;
Her staring eyes a tale
Of tragedy so great no pen
Can paint her soul's travail.

The stirring stories told of men
Who fought and won new land
From its primeval enemies
Forget that in the band

Were women torn by pain and grief
Who stood staunch by man's side
Upheld by naught that spurred him on,
Adventure—conquest—pride.

A woman's way, to long for peace,
A man's, to long for war;
A woman's lot to sacrifice
For man, the conqueror.

The woman in the wagon fought
Her silent fight alone;
The grim renunciation of
Her people—children—home.

Oh, pioneers, you valiant men!
Would you have stood the test—
Without the woman in the wagon,
Would you have won the West?

Clyde Robertson, *They Rise Accusing* (New York: Henry Harrison, 1930), pp. 13-15. Reprinted by special permission of the author.

THE HOME WINNER

By Gene Lindberg

In this celebration of pioneer women, the "prophets" who needed women for fulfillment of their dreams are the religious leaders of the Mormons who settled in Utah. This poem was reprinted in *Pioneer Songs,* compiled by the Daughters of the Utah Pioneers in 1940.

Prophets, gazing toward the mountains,
Once foresaw a promised land.
They saw fields in desert valleys,
They saw mighty cities stand
On the hills. But all their dreaming
Would not find fulfillment, now,
Had the hand that rocked the cradle
Lacked the strength to guide the plow.

Men who battled single-handed,
With unbroken wilderness,
Staggered back at last defeated
By the curse of loneliness.
Men made trails for men to follow
When adventure bade them roam,
But the trail a woman followed
Led, unerring, toward a home.

Home! No price of toil and patience
Was too great for her to pay.
Danger, suffering and hardship—
Thru them all she found a way.
Her indomitable courage
Banished doubt and conquered fear.
She was mother, wife and partner—
Every inch a pioneer.

From the Denver *Post,* May 3, 1931. Reprinted by special permission of the author.

LAY OF THE LAST FRONTIER

By Harold Hersey

The West remains proud of its highly colored memories of high, hard, and dangerous living. The following roll call of famous good men and bad men arouses many memories.

Hickok rests by Calamity Jane,
John Hardin sleeps in thuh dust,
Billy thuh Kid's fast forty-fours
Are toys long silent with rust.

Pat Garrett is only a memory,
Buffalo Bill a name,
Joseph Smith and Brigham Young
Wrapped in sheets of flame.

Cummings and Dallas Stoudenmire,
Middaugh and McCarthy are still,
Custer along thuh Little Big Horn,
Marshall of Sutter's Mill.

McLoughlin—"White Eagle" of Oregon,
Erickson's "longest" bar,
The Mississippi pilots pass,
And Nelson of thuh "Star."

Thuh heroes of thuh Alamo,
Mark Twain and good Bill Nye,
Artemus Ward and Uncle Abe,
Last Chance Gulch and "Chi."

"Marshall's" of Bret Harte's "'Frisco" days
Where met a dyin' race;
Jack London, Sterling, Ambrose Bierce
At Papa Coppa's place.

Sibley, monarch of old St. Paul,
Cole Younger, Jesse James. . . .

Rollin' forth from thuh throat of Time
In a thunderin' roster of names.

Thuh beat of thuh buffalo down thuh plains,
Thuh Remington's sharp report
When wheelin' out of a cloud of dust
They shot 'em down for sport.

They have laid away thuh uniforms
Of Eighteen-Forty-Eight,
And in place of thuh Alamo "defi"
We argue and hesitate.

The settler watchin' in thuh night
With sharp, suspended breath,
For Redskins etched ag'inst thuh sky
In silhouettes of death.

Rain-In-The-Face and Sittin' Bull
Have gone their ways at last,
And all thuh other chieftains are
But shadows on thuh past.

Along with Santa Anna's leg
Have gone thuh wounds of war,
With thuh clotted blood of thuh Wilderness
In Eighteen-Sixty-Four.

Valhalla's halls are echoin'
With those who laughed at fear,
And all thuh host who rode thuh range
Now ride thuh Last Frontier.

Harold Hersey, *Singing Rawhide, a Book of Western Ballads* (New York: George H. Doran Co., 1926), pp. 185-189.

V

THE GREAT OUTDOORS

THE DUST OF THE OVERLAND TRAIL

By James Barton Adams

The natural beauties of the West were first seen under difficulties
by the settlers who pressed into the Rocky Mountain country.

O'er the wide-spreading plans rolled the emigrant trains
 In the stirring old pioneer days
When the ripples of heat danced on shimmering feet
 'Neath the summer sun's quivering blaze,
And the brave light that broke from each valiant eye spoke
 Of a courage that never would quail
As the hardy men pressed toward the goal in the West
 In the dust of the Overland Trail.

From the day they arose o'er the bluffs that inclose
 The historic Missouri's dark tide,
And the slow-moving trains headed west o'er the plains
 There were perils on every side.
With their eyes gleaming hate painted foes lay in wait
 In the brush of the gulch and the swale,
But the heroes pressed on for the prize to be won
 In the dust of the Overland Trail.

Oh! how glad was their song as they journeyed along
 When the peaks of the range met their eyes—
When the snow line so white caught their wondering sight
 As a beacon of peace in the skies.
And their joy was untold as the gray schooners rolled
 Through the winding Platte's beautiful vale,
And their lips fashioned jests as they beat from their breasts
 The dust of the Overland Trail.

Sons of Colorado, vol. 1, no. 10 (March, 1907), p. 21.

SILHOUETTE IN SEPIA

By Robert V. Carr

Resting at night, the emigrant on his way to becoming a pioneer got a taste of vastness and beauty.

> The camp's asleep and thro' the gloom,
> The white-topped wagons spectral loom;
> And weird the lonesome coyotes call,
> And quiet stars stand watch o'er all.
> The fire's down—the shadows creep,
> Their work is done—the camp's asleep.

Robert V. Carr, *Black Hills Ballads* (Denver: The Reed Publishing Co., 1902), p. 113.

NEW MEXICO AND ARIZONA

By Pvt. George Canterbury

Those who made the overland journey by foot and wagon—even the Mormons—groused like soldiers. Some were soldiers. The author of one record of a transcontinental journey asks: "Would you like an enumeration of the main attractions of our March? Here is one by George Canterbury, private, Company C,—Regiment Cavalry:"

> Fierce Mars I bid a glad farewell,
> And turn my back upon Bellona,
> To photograph, in doggerel,
> New Mexico and Arizona:
>
> The stinging grass, the thorny plants,
> And other prickly, tropic glories:
> The thieving, starved inhabitants,
> Who look so picturesque in stories;
>
> The dusty, hot, long, dreary way,
> Where 'neath a blazing sun you totter,
> To reach a camp at close of day,
> And find it destitute of water;

The dying mule, the dried-up spring,
    Which novel-writers seldom notice;
The song the blood mosquitoes sing,
    The vicious howling of coyotes;

Tarantulas and centipedes,
    Horned toads, and piercing mesquite daggers,
With thorny bushes, grass, and weeds,
    To bleed the traveller as he staggers.

Why paint things in a rosy light,
    And never tell the simple fact?—thus,
How one sits down to rest at night,
    And often squats upon a cactus.

The night bird's music, sweet and clear,
    Is over-pictured not a *leetle;*
A search might prove the enchanter's ear
    The habitation of a beetle.

And oft at night the sentinel
    Who, dozing, dreams of distant battle,
Is roused in fright to hear the yell
    Of Indians who have nipped his cattle.

There is no fairer rule than that
    Which gives to Caesar all that's Caesar's,
Yet this is not a land of fat
    Because the people are called Greasers.

"And so on, for quantity, through fifty verses. The picture must be truthful, for he adds:"

If any think me too severe,
    Or call my yarn a wicked libel,
I'll take, to prove myself sincere,
    My 'davy'—on a Mormon Bible.

Quoted in James F. Meline, *Two Thousand Miles on Horseback* (New York: Hurd and Houghton, 1867), pp. 262-263.

OUT WHERE THE WEST BEGINS

By *Arthur Chapman*

But the "booster" approach to western scenery quickly displaced the fervent, profane comments of the sun-baked emigrant. Widely quoted is Arthur Chapman's paean, first published as part of his daily column, eventually the stepping-stone on which he rose to become rich, famous, and an Easterner. Within five years after its appearance, this was perhaps the best-known bit of verse in America.

> Out where the hand-clasp's a little stronger,
> Out where the smile dwells a little longer,
> That's where the West begins;
> Out where the sun is a little brighter,
> Where the snows that fall are a trifle whiter,
> Where the bonds of home are a wee bit tighter,
> That's where the West begins.
>
> Out where the skies are a little bluer,
> Out where friendship's a little truer,
> That's where the West begins;
> Out where a fresher breeze is blowing,
> Where there's laughter in every streamlet flowing,
> Where there's more of reaping and less of sowing,
> That's where the West begins.
>
> Out where the world is in the making,
> Where fewer hearts in despair are aching,
> That's where the West begins;
> Where there's more of singing and less of sighing,
> Where there's more of giving and less of buying,
> And a man makes friends without half trying—
> That's where the West begins.

From *The Denver Republican,* December 3, 1911.

THE MAN OF THE OPEN WEST

By Arthur W. Monroe

Poems like Chapman's and this one have established a conception of the Westerner founded on considerable historical truth and still enduring—in part because the living Westerner is impressed by this ideal.

When the glow of fading sunlight,
　　Gives way to gath'ring dark,
A lone campfire's glowing embers,
　　Release gold-gleaming sparks;
A man sits in the deep shadows,
　　In a posture of rest—
He's a man of rugged ranges,
　　Man of the open West.

He's ridden atop the springtime,
　　He's scorched in summer heat;
He has known Old Winter's scourging,
　　By frozen hands and feet,
Without a sign of a whimper,
　　He long has faced the test;
He's a true son of the ranges,
　　Man of the open West.

A face that is tan and freckled,
　　Stubby beard on his chin;
A chest that is broad and muscled,
　　And heart that's true within;
His legs are strong and sturdy built,
　　Bowed a bit at the best,
This son of the rugged ranges—
　　Man of the open West.

His doors are open to strangers,
　　Alone in his big land;
Many a heart has been made glad,
　　By the clasp of his hand.

In his face reflects the spirit,
    By firelight's glow caressed—
Spirit of the rugged ranges,
    Soul of the open West.

Arthur W. Monroe, *Sunshine and Shadows* (Montrose, Colorado: The Press Printing Co., 1927), p. 10. Reprinted by special permission of the author.

COLORADO

By John D. Dillenback

Patriotism for state areas, defined arbitrarily by surveyors' lines, grows intense.

Thou hast thine eyrie in the lifted lands,
    O Colorado, mountain-born and free;
    Unvexed by terrors of the far-off sea,
On earth's high crest thy favored realm expands.

Nature bestowed thy dower with lavish hands,
    The richest gifts within her treasury,
    Which from creation she reserved for thee,
Thy ore-veined mountains and thy golden sands.

Far eastward, ocean-vast, thy plains extend;
Westward thy snow-crowned mountains meet the sky;
    Heavens of unclouded blue above thee bend,
And the bright sun looks on thee lovingly.
    To what God hath so wrought may great souls lend
The fadeless luster of achievements high.

From *Evenings with Colorado Poets,* compiled and edited by Francis S. Kinder and F. Clarence Spencer (Denver: The World Press, Inc., 1894 and 1926), p. 9.

LAND WHERE THE COLUMBINES GROW

By Arthur J. Fynn

The columbine is Colorado's state flower. A Denver educator wrote the following hymn of praise, which was adopted as the state song by the 1915 Legislature.

Where the snowy peaks gleam in the moonlight,
  Above the dark forests of pine,
And the wild foaming waters dash onward
  Toward lands where the tropic stars shine;
Where the scream of the bold mountain eagle
  Responds to the notes of the dove
Is the purple-robed West, the land that is best,
  The pioneer land that we love.

CHORUS

'Tis the land where the columbines grow,
Overlooking the plains far below,
While the cool summer breeze
In the evergreen trees
Softly sings where the columbines grow.

The bison is gone from the upland,
  The deer from the canon has fled,
The home of the wolf is deserted,
  The antelope moans for his dead,
The war-whoop re-echoes no longer,
  The Indian's only a name,
And the nymphs of the grove in their loneliness rove
  But the columbine blooms just the same.

Let the violet brighten the brookside
  In the sunlight of earlier spring,
Let the clover bedeck the green meadow
  In the days when the orioles sing;

Let the goldenrod herald the autumn,
But under the midsummer sky,
In its fair western home may the columbine bloom
Till our great mountain rivers run dry.

From *Evenings with Colorado Poets*, compiled and edited by Francis S. Kinder and F. Clarence Spencer (Denver: The World Press, Inc., 1894 and 1926), p. 127.

LINES ON MOUNTAIN VILLAGES
By *"Sunset Joe"*

Set in mighty scenery, many small towns in the Rockies can claim grandeur.

O wondrous scene is Meeker,
    Where rims of ranges frown,
Rewards await the seeker
    In Alamosa's town.
Famed Creede by icy river,
    Is praised both far and wide,
Montrose blessed by the Giver,
    Grander still, is Telluride.

A lovely picture is Boulder,
    Bewitching in delight,
With Aspen 'neath the shoulder,
    Of azure mountain bright.
Salida is a city,
    In every way unique,
And Crested Butte is pretty,
    Near by to snowy peak.

Red Mountain's mystic story,
    With Rico's golden vale,
Also recalls the glory,
    Of Silverton's steep trail.
Enchanted La Veta ever,
    Far Monte Vista too,

While Buena Vista never
Will be lost to our view.

When choosing by selection,
Our hearts alone obey,
For us there is perfection,
In only fair Ouray.
Divinest hope abounding,
Gem of the Golden West;
Our tributes are resounding,
For the village we love best.

"Sunset Joe," the Poet of the Southwest, *The Natural Beauty and Grandeur of Ouray, Colorado, and the San Juan District in Verse,* compiled and printed by *The Ouray Herald* (n.d.), p. 33.

RIVERS OF THE WEST

By "Sunset Joe"

The roll of Colorado streams makes a sonorous addition to the index of American names.

The La Plata chants silver
Where its glittering waters roll,
Melodies of dreamy romance
Bring repose unto the soul.
While meandering down the valley
Rio Dolores, grief to cast,
As the ancient River Lethe,
All oblivion of the past.

Rio Blanco sings in rapture
Of blue lakes with sporting fish,
San Miguel, of health and treasure,
Best of wealth that one could wish.
Rio Grande is delighting,
Tells of Monte Vista's Vale,
Roaring Fork in icy leaping,
Softly whispers: "Carbondale."

193

Yampa moans in forlorn cadence
    Of red walls and temples grand,
And the San Juan, lost and lonely,
    Of the rainbow bridges' land.
Mancos, of cliff-dwellers' ruins,
    Indians, Navajos and Utes,
While in far Utah, Green River
    Weirdly drones of castled buttes.

Eagle River cries in freedom,
    As an eaglet from the nest,
Colorado's flashing ripplets,
    El Dorado, Golden West
Roars in anger—fiercely warning,
    Gunnison, Black Canyon doom,
And Rio de Las Animas
    Echoes dark despair and gloom.

Symphonies of Rio Los Pinos
    Woo the balm of scented pines,
Florida's concert of flower-songs
    Caress the purple columbines.
Huerfano of Huajatolla
    Mourns in spirit-haunted glades,
And Conejos, lisping, wailing,
    Races in swift white cascades.

Not so, Uncompahgre River
    In its mountain chasm deep,
Sometimes glad, yet sadly sighing,
    Often mystically to weep.
For its wavelets, murmuring splashing,
    Tender lyrics thus convey,
No vale kissed by laughing waters,
    Can be lovely as Ouray.

"Sunset Joe," the Poet of the Southwest, *The Natural Beauty and Grandeur of Ouray, Colorado, and the San Juan District in Verse.* compiled and printed by *The Ouray Herald* (n.d.), pp. 5-6.

CHEYENNE MOUNTAIN

By Helen Hunt Jackson

This sonnet, by the nationally famous "H. H.," a health-seeker in Colorado in 1873, indicates the influence of transcendental romanticism on Rocky Mountain poets, an influence still apparent in much contemporary verse.

By easy slope to west as if it had
No thought, when first its soaring was begun,
Except to look devoutly to the sun,
It rises and has risen, until glad,
With light as with a garment, it is clad,
Each dawn, before the tardy plains have won
One ray; and after day has long been done
For us, the light doth cling reluctant, sad to leave its brow.
   Beloved mountain, I
Thy worshipper as thou the sun's each morn
My dawn, before the dawn, receive from thee;
And think, as thy rose-tinted peaks I see
That thou wert great when Homer was not born.
And ere thou change all human song shall die!

"H. H." in the *New York Independent*, July 31, 1879, included in Helen Hunt Jackson, *Poems* (Boston: Roberts Bros., 1893), p. 258.

TO PIKES PEAK

By Elijah Clarence Hills

Another Colorado Springs poet found materials for the following verse sermon in the mighty mass of stone called Pikes Peak and in its primeval brooks. A reader may, of course, enjoy the description and ignore the moralizing.

Thou hast clothed thy steepest hillsides
   With the fragrant fir and pine,
With the timid quaking-aspen,
   And the pale-blue columbine;

195

And thy torrents downward rushing
From the melting snow o'erhead,
Bring a tender, plaintive music
To the canyon's deep-worn bed.

Thou art ever changing color
In thy coat of many hues,
From the glowing orange-crimsons
To the darkling greens and blues;
When the sun through rift in cloudland
Floods thee with his golden rays
On thy slopes the purple shadows
Flit across the browns and grays.

When thy darkened form is outlined
In the rosy western sky,
From the far-flung broken ridges
Magic castles rise on high,—
Castles with fantastic towers
Where the elf-king becks and calls,
While the evening's dying splendor
Streams between the blackened walls.

When the lightning's fiery serpent
Cleaves the air with sudden flash,
And the startled hills give answer
To the thunder's jarring crash,
Calm and fair thy sun-kissed summit
Looms above the mist and rain,
And to thee the melting storm-clouds
Seem a white and fleecy plain.

Fold on fold thy wrinkled foothills,
Rising, lifting up to thee,
Seem the heaving, wind-tossed billows
Of a vast, tumultous sea,—
Thou, a stolid, massive island
With the uplands bare and bleak,
With the hollows and abysses,
And thy lofty, granite peak.

* * * * *

Round thee surged the moving waters
    When thou first didst lift thy head;
Thou wert then a rocky island
    In the ocean's shifting bed;
But before thy slow uprising
    Fled the sullen, restless sea,
As the mists of early morning
    From the growing sunlight flee.

Thou hast seen the floodgates loosened
    In these arid, burning skies;
Thou hast heard the palm-tree rustle
    Where the northern fir-tree sighs;
Nature at thy feet hath fashioned
    Many forms in living clay;
Some she held in fond affection;
    Some she spurned and cast away.

Last of all was Man created,
    Slower than the hare and hind,
Weaker than the bear or panther,
    But endowed with cunning mind;
Man alone knew good and evil
    And could call things by their name;
But, alas! with greater knowledge
    Followed greater sin and shame.

*   *   *   *   *

Oh, majestic, mighty mountain,
    Mocking Time's eternal flow,
When thou lookest on the mortals
    As they toil and weep below,
Dost thou think to live forever,
    Since of granite frame thou art,
While the life of Man is measured
    By the beating of his heart?

As the ancient, moss-grown boulder
    Scorns the limpid, rippling stream,
Thou dost view the flight of ages
    As an idly changing dream;

But if water ever running
    Wears the rock it rushes past,
So shall Time, the all-consuming,
    Eat away thine heart at last.

Though all matter be immortal,
    It is ever changing shape;
Soil that gives the ruddy apple,
    Gives the luscious, purple grape;
Water makes the curling vapor,
    Floating ice and drifting snow;
And the rock that forms the mountain
    Makes the sandy plain below.

Death is but a changed condition;
    Life is but a passing show;
Sea and mountain, earth and heaven,
    Come, and pause a while, and go.
Length of life should not be reckoned
    By the number of the years;
Less an age of senseless matter
    Than an hour of love and tears!

Elijah Clarence Hills, editor, *The Pikes Peak Region in Song and Myth* (Colorado Springs: Colorado College Publication, General Lines 66, 1913), pp. 183-186.

PIKES PEAK

Anonymous

In frontier writing, a sense of humor saved many an admirer of nature from "low grade mysticism."

I'm looking at your lofty head
    Away up in the air.
Eight thousand feet above the plain
    Where grows the prickly-pear.
A great big thing with ice on,
    You seem to be up there.

Away above the timber-line
    You lift your frosty head,
Where lightnings are engendered;
    And thunderstorms are bred;
But you'd be a bigger tract of land
    If you were thin out-spread.

Quoted in A. A. Hayes, *New Colorado and the Santa Fe Trail* (New York: Harper & Brothers, 1880), p. 52.

UTE PASS

By Ernest Whitney

Romantic poets have often brought figures of classical mythology to the Wild West. This is one of the happier instances of such transplanting.

Vast corridor through Nature's roofless halls,
Pike beckons welcome far across the land
To this sole gateway through its granite walls,
By chaos wrought with harsh primeval hand.

He scarred his pathway through the frightful chasm
With shattered ledge and splintered crag in air,
And cliffs that writhe as though, in torturing spasm,
Some hideous monster met the Gorgon's stare.

But only once he through the ravine stormed,
While year by year roamed Beauty in the path,
And wheresoe'er she stept, that spot transformed
Bears her soft smile amid his work of wrath.

Elijah Clarence Hills, editor, *The Pikes Peak Region in Song and Myth* (Colorado Springs: Colorado College, 1913), p. 197.

BIG THOMPSON CANON

By Jean Milne Gower

Nostalgia for the wide-open spaces is usually a part of the romantic admiration of nature. Once remote, Big Thompson Canyon now is threaded by a much-traveled auto road to Estes Park; and where the Canyon widens, cottages for summer vacationers line both banks of the river.

I knew you long before great motors buzzed
    Like racing bumblebees along your roads;
Before small cots grew into busy hives
    Where narrow vales have tempted new abodes.
You were an awesome place in those old days
    When wagons crept along your cliffs like snails,
And, in the widened places by the creek,
    The camp was struck at night. What merry tales
Of venturous doings graced the supper hour!
    Then by the campfire's glow more tales were told
And old time songs echoed from cliff to cliff;
    While stars peeped through the pines like sparks of gold,
Dodging your rugged rimmings far aloft—
    Almost they met—then left a rift of sky
To follow the river's zig-zag course below
    Where willows drooped as he passed swiftly by.
Never can I describe those matchless nights—
    The pungent smell of pine—the stars above—
The dreamy sense of the river's ceaseless flow,
    Wooing the boulders with his Song of Love.

Jean Milne Gower, *The Kaleidoscope, Little Pictures of Colorado* (Denver: The Miles & Dryer Printing Co., 1923), p. 15.

AT TIMBER LINE

By Frank H. Mayer

This was written to accompany a colored photograph of The
Palisades, near Alpine Pass (elevation 11,510 feet), the highest point
in North America reached by traction railroad.

> The hoary mountains seem gray and cold
> > At timber line.
> And their wrinkled faces are worn and old
> > At timber line.
> Their aged temples are wan and bare
> 'Neath their silvery shock of aspen hair,
> And Time has set his seal everywhere
> > At timber line.
>
> The lordly elk in contentment roves
> > At timber line.
> And the shy deer sport in the sylvan groves
> > At timber line.
> And the grouse, affrighted, tread softly where
> In the thickets the grizzly has made his lair;
> And the big-horn bounds up the chasm's stair
> > At timber line.
>
> We are far above the old, sordid world
> > At timber line.
> With its cares and passions and woes infurled
> > At timber line.
> Is there aught in the forms of human speech
> To voice the lesson these old hills teach?
> While Heaven seems just within our reach
> > At timber line.

From *Colorado in Color and Song* (Denver: Frank S. Thayer, Publisher, 1899), p. 70.

TIMBER LINE TREES

By Jamie Sexton Holme

A striking feature of mountain landscapes is the twisted, stunted limber pines of the wind-swept ridges.

We never knew the touch of fur and feather,
The delicate fingertips of summer rain;
Only the sting of bitter merciless weather,
The shroud of sleet, the winds that warp and strain,
Within our twisted branches no birds sing
Or come to hush a hungry fledgling's cries.
Only. . . . the shadow of an eagle's wing
Falls, as he floats through pure and lonely skies.
We know the lightnings as familiar faces,
Whose searing glances leave us scorched and bowed—
Yet sometimes we may hold in brief embraces
The snowy garments of a wandering cloud;
And on these branches where no birds will nest
There falls the shadow of an eagle's breast.

Jamie Sexton Holme, *Floodmark* (New York: Henry Harrison, 1930),
p. 44. Reprinted by special permission of Peter Hagner Holme.

MOUNTAIN EVENINGS

By Jamie Sexton Holme

The beauty of the close of day and the coming of night are different in the mountains and yet, in meaning, the same as everywhere.

Sunset; and the mountain tops are afire.
The tall chill peaks in their trappings of ice and snow
Are burning red as a Viking's funeral pyre.
Even the glaciers flame and shimmer and glow.

Twilight; violet shadows on plain and hill.
Through green meadows, whistling, a cowherd passes.
Lazily lifting their feet through deep rich grasses
The cows turn homeward; homeward the late birds fly.

Beast and bird turn homeward, and shadows die.
Dusk; in the darkening west a faint glow lingers.
Low and rosy bright hangs the evening star,
Caught in a tiptoeing pine's long delicate fingers.
The voice of the river is crystal-thin and faint and far.

Night; and silence brims the cup of the world,
So full that one trembling drop more would spill over.
Only a moth stirs in the drowsy stillness.
Only a velvet moth, a small shy rover,
Brushes my cheek like a wind-blown wandering petal—
Brushes my cheek like a flower, and then is gone.

There is no moon tonight, she has fled to some heavenly cover.
Quenched in a sea of cloud, the stars are dim as a glow-worm's spark.
Now turns the bird to its mate, and lover to lover;
Now in the chill ravine the doe creeps close to her fawn.
Close and safe in the sheltering dark,
The dark that is kind to nest and lover,
They sleep, and wait for the dawn.

Jamie Sexton Holme, *Floodmark* (New York: Henry Harrison, 1930),
p. 45. Reprinted by special permission of Peter Hagner Holme.

THE RUINED CABIN

By Alfred Castner King

Abandoned mining towns and isolated cabins left when a pioneer
died or went away have given western scenery its romantic ruins.

There's a pathos in the solemn desolation
    Of the mountain cabin sinking in decay,
With its threshold overgrown with vegetation,
    With its door unhinged and mouldering away.
There's a weird and most disconsolate expression
    In the sashless windows with their vacant stare,
As in mute appeal, or taciturn confession
    Of a wild and inconsolable despair.

With its ridgepole bent and broken in the centre,
   From its roof of dirt and weight of winter snows;
Where the only voice to greet you as you enter
   Is the wind which down the crumbling fireplace blows;
Where the chipmunk chatters in loquacious wonder,
   As unwonted steps invade his solitude;
Where the mountain rat secretes his varied plunder
   In the chimney corners, primitive and rude.

Where the spider spins his web in grim seclusion,
   To entrap the fly and vacillating moth;
From the rotten floor, in poisonous profusion
   Spring the toad stools, with their foul and fungous growth.
Void of symmetry and semblance of equation,
   Through the chinkless cracks, the silvery moon and stars
And the sun, at each matutinal invasion,
   Shine as through a dismal dungeon's grated bars.

But no predatory hand in wanton malice
   Hath in vandal hour this dereliction wrought,
But the hand which crumbles pyramid and palace,
   The hand of Time with rust and ruin fraught;
Thus the proud or unpretentious habitation
   Shall succumb to age and melancholy mould;
All are subject to the same distintegration,
   For the occupant and house alike grow old.

Alfred Castner King, *The Passing of the Storm and Other Poems* (New York: Fleming H. Revell Co., 1907), pp. 123-124.

SPRING SONG OF ASPENS

By Lilian White Spencer

Spring is not a flamboyant season in "colorful Colorado"; its few, uncertain evidences are, therefore, treasured even more highly by the poet.

They tinkle laughter at the solemn hills,
These dryad whisperers;
Mayhap, interpreters
Of miracles with which young April thrills;
Who babble gayly as the new waked rills,
And are the harbingers
Of zephyr roisterers
That revel, drunk on wine blithe May distills.
As dainty ballet girls
In pale-green skirted twirls;
White slender limbs agleam; they dance all day
With sunbeams in a blue-arched house of play.
The merry vagabonds
Deck them with diamonds.

Ashimmer from the valleys to the snow,
Like children, mischievous,
They climb the hazardous
Steep ways and chatter, chatter, as they go.
What is the lovely secret that they know—
Wood nymphs so venturous
And frail, and tremulous
With quivering delight from top to toe:
The bright leaves, fluttering,
Are argent bells that swing
Some mystic high rejoicing to command:
Such chimes were surely cast in fairyland.
June's ecstacy are these
That men call aspen trees!

Lilian White Spencer, *Arrowheads* (New York: The Parade Publishing Co., 1929), p. 37. Reprinted by special permission of the author.

NIGHT ON THE PRAIRIE

By Rufus B. Sage

These sonnets were written by a man who wandered with the fur traders over the plains and prairies and up into the Black Hills, from 1841 to 1844. They offer another instance of the impact of hitherto unknown spaces and scenery upon "genteel" nineteenth century culture.

I

The sable garb of darkness clothes the land,
    And twilight's sickly hue bids day farewell;
The prairie's vast expanse on either hand
    Marks solitude's domain. O'er hill and dell,
And wide-extended plain, I cast my eyes,
    To view, perchance, some grove or fav'ring stream
    And hie me thitherward while yet the gleam
Of day's fast-falling light bepaints the skies
    With tints scarce seen,—for there I'd seek repose,—
But for them look in vain, so here, alone,
    Wearied and worn, I sit me down and close
My tiresome wanderings,—nor bate to own
    The chilling thrill of terror o'er me creeps,
    And from my mind all thoughts of slumber keeps!

II

Oh, Solitude! First-born of Night! 'Tis here
    Thy reign is undisputed! Here no noise
Of human feet doth greet thy list'ning ear,—
    Save chance as mine, or savage want enjoys
His arms at chase or rage at bloody war!—
    Here haunts the beast of prey. The starved wolf's howl
    In ceaseless concert swells! The midnight owl
Joins in his dolesome lay;—the raven's caw
    Loud mingles with the panther's yell,—and then
The hoarse-toned bison grunts his bass, and makes
    Thy dismal realm more drear to lonely men.
Aeolus here his fresh-form'd wind awakes,
    And marks its speed unchecked; whose whistling moan
    O'er thy domain makes loneliness more lone!

III

My thoughts, now kindred to the scene, arise
    In hurried flight, whose hideous aspects wake,
Full quick, imagination's sleepless eyes,
    That conjure up such frightful forms as shake
The boldest hearts with dread. In every herb
    Of prouder growth,—whose prongs the sweeping blast
    Hath taught to move,—some ice of savage cast
Appears and threatens ill, as if to curb
    The onward progress of the god of sleep:—
(For here man sees his fellow man, unknown,
    As foe; and, arm'd for fight, he minds to keep
The strictest watch, lest, from advantage shown,
    He tempt unlucky war.) So hurriedly
    I snatch my arms to fight each form I see!

IV

But why thus fear? Give place, ye visions dread!
    Ye thoughts of boding danger, drearisome,
Cease to oppress! Is not the path I tread
    So by Omniscience mark'd, that perils come
Not near, to even hurt a single hair,
    Without His wise permit? Are not my days
    Securely meted out, and all my ways
So guarded, too, that thronging dangers share
    No part in harm's advance or death's progress
Till all are told? And can my vigilance,
    Father'd by childish fear, make more or less
The given sum? Cheerily, draw courage thence,
    My cowering heart; feel safety here. Give room
    To other thoughts, and chase these clouds of gloom.

V

Thus, banished fear, at reason's bid, I cast
    My willing gaze toward heaven. In every star
That forms the sparkling crown of night, though fast
    In regions of unbounded space, so far
As scarcely seen by mortal ken,—appears
    Some guardian angel, robed in light, to keep
    His ceaseless vigils o'er my couch of sleep,

Lest in my slumbering moments danger near
  To cut the thread of life, and thus undo
The purposes of God. The silver moon
  Sheds forth her radiance unconfined, and through
The desert wild to flower and herb gives boon,
  And decks each blade with dewy pearls, and pours
  Then on the earth, to cheer my waking hours.

VI

Nature's vast caravansers, above,
  Below, around, on either side, begirt
With midnight's varied splendors, scenes I love,
  Becomes enchantment's self, while zephyrs sport
The fragrance of the wild-flowers multiform,
  And greet my nostrils with their rich perfume,
  To please my senses. Thus my thoughts resume
Their wonted course, and hush the passing storm
  Of fear. Alone! Not lonely I. For here
E'en loneliness companion proves to me,
  And solitude is company. My ear
Drinks music from these savage sounds; I see
  Amusements in these forms; my heart's as strong,
  And easy beats, as 'mid a city's throng!

VII

To me thrice welcome then, ye prairies wild!
  Midnight, and gloom, and solitude, ye please
My restless fancy! Welcome then your child!—
  For here's my home. And so with mind at ease,
I will embrace my mother earth, and court
  The soothing power of sleep. The clear blue sky
  My canopy, the ground my bed, I lie
Encurtain'd by the pale moon-beams, which sport
  Beside my lowly couch, and light the dew
With mimic diamonds' glow while flowers around
  My pillow'd head their willing incense strew,
And the sweet dreaming bird anon doth sound
  Some isolated note of melody!—
  Thus chamber'd here, may not kings envy me?

Rufus B. Sage, *Rocky Mountain Adventures* (Dayton, Ohio: Edward Canby, n.d.; original edition, Philadelphia, 1846), pp. 332-334.

SIMPSON'S REST

By George S. Simpson

One of the early settlers of the Rocky Mountain area was buried, at his own request as expressed in this poem, in a tomb cut in solid rock near Trinidad, Colorado.

Lay me to rest on yon towering height
Where the silent cloud shadows glide—
Where solitude holds its slumberous reign
Far away from the human tide.

I fain would sleep near the old pine tree
That looks down the valley below,
Like a soldier guarding a comrade's grave,
Or a sentinel watching the foe.

'Twas a refuge once, in the bygone time.
When a pitiful fate was near,
When my days were young and full of love
For a life I held too dear.

Through all the long years that have passed away
Since that night of storm and dread
I've prayed that the boughs that sheltered me then
Might wave o'er my dust when dead.

Delve deep my grave in the stern gray rock;
In its rigid embrace let me rest,
With naught but my name on the stone at my head
And the symbol of faith on my breast.

One mourner may remember where sleeps
In his rock ribbed tomb, the lone dead,
May breathe for the loved one to heaven a prayer.
A tear to his memory shed.

From *Sketches of Colorado,* edited by Will Ferril (Denver: The Western Press Bureau, 1911), p. 19.

THE WANDERER'S GRAVE

By Rufus B. Sage

While journeying over the plains, Rufus B. Sage's party lost one of its number by death. After helping to bury this companion in a lonely grave Sage "felt like giving vent to my feeling in verse." The following poem resulted.

> Away from friends, away from home
> And all the heart holds dear,
> A weary wand'rer laid him down, —
> Nor kindly aid was near.
>
> And sickness prey'd upon his frame
> And told its tale of woe,
> While sorrow mark'd his pallid cheeks
> And sank his spirit low.
>
> Nor waiting friends stood round his couch
> A healing to impart, —
> Nor human voice spoke sympathy,
> To sooth his aching heart.
>
> The stars of night his watchers were, —
> His fan the rude winds breath,
> And while they sigh'd their hollow moans,
> He closed his eyes in death.
>
> Upon the prairie's vast expanse
> This weary wand'rer lay;
> And far from friends, and far from home,
> He breath'd his life away!
>
> A lovely valley marks the spot
> That claims his lowly bed;
> But o'er the wand'rer's hapless fate
> No friendly tear was shed.
>
> No willing grave received the corpse
> Of this poor lonely one; —

His bones, alas, were left to bleach
And moulder 'neath the sun!

The night-wolf howl'd his requiem,—
The rude winds danced his dirge;
And e'er anon, in mournful chime,
Sigh'd forth the mellow surge!

The Spring shall teach the rising grass
To twine for him a tomb;
And, o'er the spot where he doth lie,
Shall bid the wild flowers bloom.

But, far from friends, and far from home
Ah, dismal thought, to die!
Oh, let me 'mid my friends expire,
And with my fathers lie.

Rufus B. Sage, *Rocky Mountain Adventures* (Dayton, Ohio: Edward
Canby, n.d.; original edition, Philadelphia, 1846), pp. 93-94.

THE WANDERER

By Eugene Field

The pranksome Field, in one of his serious moments, expressed
the sense of exile which many a settler has felt in the new land.

Upon a mountain's height, far from the sea,
I found this shell,
And to my curious ear this lonely thing
Ever a song of ocean seemed to sing—
Ever a tale of ocean seemed to tell.

How came this shell upon the mountain height?
Ah, who can say
Whether there dropped by some too careless hand—
Whether there cast when oceans swept the land
Ere the Eternal had ordained the Day.

Strange was it not? Far from its native sea,
    One song it sang—
Sang of the mighty mysteries of the tide—
Sang of the awful, vast profound and wide—
    Softly with echoes of the ocean rang.

And as the shell upon the mountain's height
    Sings of the sea,
So do I ever, leagues and leagues away—
So do I ever, wandering where I may,
    Sing, O my home—sing, O my home, of thee.

Eugene Field, *A Little Book of Western Verse* (New York: Charles Scribner's Sons, 1889), pp. 75-76.

SUMMER ON THE GREAT AMERICAN DESERT

By Rufus B. Sage

There are, today, those who find the plains as appealing as the mountains. Irrigation and improved methods of dry farming have transformed much of the area once called "The Great American Desert" into prosperous and attractive communities. But when Sage made his trips West, in 1841-44, he found "almost the entire expanse from the Arkansas to the Gulf of Mexico . . . little else than a vast desert of barrenness," worthy of the following verse description.

Ye dreary plains, that round me lie,
    So parch'd with summer's heat,
No more ye please my wand'ring eye,
    Or woo my weary feet.

Why hath the spring your beauty borne
    Into his hiding place,
And left the widow'd winds to mourn
    The charms they would embrace?

Why should those flowers, whose honey'd breath
    With incense filled the breeze,
Drooping and wither'd, lie in death,
    And now no longer please?

212

That grassy carpet, green and wide,
    Why turn'd to stubble now?
Save 'chance along some streamlet's side,
    Where less'ning waters flow!

And why those gently murm'ring rills,
    Whose soft melodious strains
Were wont to echo 'mong the hills
    No longer reach the plains?

The lark no longer meets the morn,—
    Nor linnet pours his throat,—
Nor feather'd warbler hails the dawn
    With his sweet, mellow note;—

Nor even insect cheers the scene,
    Where Solitude alone,
In wither'd garb, as Desert Queen,
    Rears her eternal throne!

These thirsty plains, with open mouth,
    Implore the gentle shower;
But vainly plead, while summer's drouth
    In scorching heat doth pour!

Nor grateful shade, of spreading tree,
    Invites my feet to rest;
Nor cooling stream, in melody,
    Attempts my quicken'd zest.

So dismal all! why should I stay
    And sicken by their view?
Thrice gladly will I turn away,
    And bid these scenes adieu!

Rufus B. Sage, *Rocky Mountain Adventures* (Dayton, Ohio: Edward Canby, n.d.; original edition, Philadelphia, 1846), p. 313.

THE TOLL OF THE DESERT

By Arthur W. Monroe

Of course there are desert spaces in the West where it doesn't pay to travel without proper equipment and supplies. A few have gone out but never returned.

This is the toll of the desert,
 These bleaching bones in the sun;
Ever the price of its gruelling,
 If all its treasures are won.

Stern is the sway of the desert,
 Ever and always the same;
The strong and the sturdy survive it,
 But woe to the weak and lame.

These bleaching bones on the hillside
 Bear witness for others to see,
Where someone has paid the ransom,
 The desert's toll and its fee.

Take heed from this gruesome warning,
 Take care lest you might stay too,
To bleach on the sands of the desert,
 And the coyotes howl over you.

Arthur W. Monroe, *Sunshine and Shadows* (Montrose, Colorado: The Press Printing Co., 1927), p. 12. Reprinted by special permission of the author.

THE RATTLESNAKE

By Robert V. Carr

The rattlesnake is a native of the arid regions, feared and hated by all. In some communities rattlesnake hunts are organized each spring in the attempt to exterminate this "foe to man."

> O'er sunbaked plains he winds his way,
> Slow squirms his glittering length along;
> And from the sage brush sanded gray,
> Doth come his fearful warning song.
> Watch, watch for him, his sting is death,
> And in those angry, flaming eyes
> Doth lurk the awful hate of years.
>
> Sunning where the barren bluffs arise,
> He lies in lazy coil. The scaly lid
> Doth curtain o'er those vengeful eyes;
> Doth hold their murderous fire hid—
> When lo, a step is heard, the horrid head
> Is swiftly reared, and keen he sounds
> A challenge full of deathless hate.

Robert V. Carr, *Black Hills Ballads* (Denver: The Reed Publishing Co., 1902), p. 121.

THE SUN DROPS RED

By Nellie Burget Miller

The horror of drought in the "Dust Bowl" is relieved only by the long-awaited rains.

> The sun drops red through a curtain of dust,
> White scars seam the alkali plain,
> No sound or motion—save over there
> A tumbleweed starts on its endless quest
> For God knows what—or where.
> The brown grass clings to the fields like rust,

But deep in my heart is the sound of rain—
The stealthy moccasined feet of the rain,
Pat, pat on the sun-baked crust;
Like dear remembered dreams of love
In sleepless nights of pain.
The sun drops red through a curtain of dust.

Nellie Burget Miller, *The Sun Drops Red* (Denver: Sage Books, 1947),
p. 4. Reprinted by special permission of the author.

A COLORADO SAND STORM

By Eugene Field

This fugitive poem by Field reflects his newspaper activity in
Denver while he was gathering a reputation, before going on to
Chicago and to fame. In most western towns and cities Main Street
is now paved, but the wind still blows occasionally.

See the madly blowing dust,
    Oh! the dust!
How it revels in the gust,
How it covers with a crust
Of tenacious, gritty must
    Every object in the street.
It is monarch of us all:
When it rises up, we fall,
    When it comes,
    When it hums,
Ev'ry kind of business flags,
Ev'ry branch of business lags,
    And it gags
    As it snags
Ev'ry class of trade afloat.
It is death to eyes and throat,
    For it kills
    As it fills
Ev'ry eye and ev'ry throat,
    Oh, the dust, dust, dust!

Yet it's useless to complain,
Intercessions are in vain,
    But it's far from being just
We should suffer so with dust,
Since the city is not bust,
    Oh, the dust,
It is here, it is there,
It is flying everywhere!
How it permeates the air!
    Oh, the dust!
    How it's cuss'd.

From *The Denver Tribune,* November 6, 1882; reprinted in *A Little Book of Tribune Verse,* edited by Joseph G. Brown (New York: Tandy, Wheeler and Co., 1901), pp. 172-173.

THE FOREST FIRE

By Arthur W. Monroe

Every summer forest rangers and volunteers from ranches and vacation resorts are forced to fight the red terror which ranges across mountain slopes and through dry grass, thick underbrush, and precious stands of timber.

Rolling clouds of greasy smoke,
    Crashing giant trees;
Roaring, flashing, fiendish flames,
    Upon an angry breeze.
Frightened, fleeing, bird and beast,
    Shrieking in despair—
The ugly demon, forest fire,
    Is on another tear.

Arthur W. Monroe, *Sunshine and Shadows* (Montrose, Colorado: The Press Printing Co., 1927), p. 32. Reprinted by special permission of the author.

LOST IN A BLIZZARD

By Arthur W. Monroe

Until late spring, snow storms in the mountains bring another terror to man and beast. Here, however, the poet provides a rescue.

Stumbling over fallen logs,
Plunging into drifts,
Seeing only whirling snow,
Fearing hidden cliffs.

Numbed with cold and feet half dead,
Dragging slowly on,
Blinded by the angry wind,
Senses almost gone.

Lost, and freezing inch by inch,
Praying for the end,
Bumping 'gainst a swaying tree?
No, it's Bill, my friend.

Arthur W. Monroe, *Sunshine and Shadows* (Montrose, Colorado: The Press Printing Co., 1927), p. 17. Reprinted by special permission of the author.

THE SNOWSTORM

By Pearl Riggs Crouch

The blizzard seen down below, through the window of a homesteading shack, affords more opportunity for contemplation of its awful majesty.

Across the plain the wind whines through the sage,
And boots the tumbleweeds with veering whim;
The day is dimming through the merging mists
And huddled herds head south against the rim.

On flurried wing the snowbirds, wheeling low,
  In shrill, staccato chorus whir away;
In vagrant gusts the snowflakes eddy by,
  And closer swirls the circling wall of gray.

Unleashed, the north wind swings his whistling whip—
  The air is blinded by a whirling veil;
And riding through the maelstrom, madly-free,
  Exultant shriek the demons of the gale!

From *Evenings with Colorado Poets*, edited by Francis S. Kinder and F. Clarence Spencer (Denver: The World Press, Inc., 1894 and 1926), p. 112.

PRAIRIE WOLVES

By Robert V. Carr

In cold, as in heat, there is animal life to remind the settler that "Nature in the raw is seldom mild."

Up where the white bluffs fringe the plain,
When heaven's lights are on the wane;
They sing their songs as demons might
Shriek wild a chorus to the night.
Gaunt, gray brutes with dripping fangs,
And eyes a-flame with hunger pangs;
With lips curled back in snarls of hate,
They wail a curse against their fate.

Robert V. Carr, *Black Hills Ballads* (Denver: The Reed Publishing Co., 1902), p. 120.

PIONEER WOMAN

By Vesta Pierce Crawford

In the poetry of the homesteader there has always been a recognition of the ever-present hardships and none of the reckless gaiety characteristic of the cowboy and the miner. Women were needed for successful homesteading; often they suffered more from loneliness than from overwork.

>Beneath these alien stars
>>In darkness I have stood alone,
>Barriers more than mountains
>>Between me and my home.

>And I have seen the shadows fall
>>Grim patterned on the floor,
>As onward passed the faces
>>Beyond the cabin door.

>The desert wind has waved my hair;
>>Desert sands have etched my face,
>And the courage of the mountains
>>Has bound me to this place.

>And something of its peace I've won,
>>Triumphant now my day is done.
>Oh, I have stood with only God
>>Between me and the sun.

From *Utah Sings*, edited by Harrison R. Merrill and Elsie T. Brandley (Provo: Utah Academy of Sciences, Arts and Letters, 1934), p. 95. Reprinted by special permission of the author.

THE SHACK

By Nellie Burget Miller

Since the homesteader had to stay on in the vastness, the heat,
and the blizzards, grimness was much of his portion. Little wonder
that a high percentage of ranch women became a bit queer.

A passing motorist glanced back:
"See how the sun lights up that little shack
with Inness gold! Painters would not dare
to give us sunset tints like those.
I wonder if that woman knows she's in a picture."
    The plains-wife peered from out her darkening door
    until the car was out of sight;
    the radiance was gone—the windows of the shack
    were like dead eyes left open wide to stare.
    About her everywhere
    silence tightened like a shell;
    a coyote's wail fell like a knife upon it,
    shattering it to bits which flew
    each to the other and grew
    into another silence
    greater than the first;
    Slowly she turned and shut the door
    against the chill . . .
    The car was gone and shifting sand
    had drifted in so soon
    and covered up its track.

Nellie Burget Miller, *The Sun Drops Red* (Denver: Sage Books, 1947),
p. 15. Reprinted by special permission of the author.

ON RECROSSING THE ROCKY MOUNTAINS
AFTER MANY YEARS

By John Charles Frémont

The famous explorer Frémont, one-time "conqueror" of California, military and political leader who had once aspired even to the presidency of the United States, saw in the winter-changed Rockies, which he was traversing in later years, a reflection of his once-brilliant but shadowed career. In rather Byronic phraseology, disillusioned Frémont expressed his despondent mood in the following poem.

Long years ago I wandered here,
In the midsummer of the year,—
    Life's summer too;
A score of horsemen here we rode,
The mountain world its glories showed,
    All fair to view.

These scenes, in glowing colors drest,
Mirrored the life within my breast,
    Its world of hopes;
The whispering woods and fragrant breeze
That stirred the grass in verdant seas
    On billowy slopes,

And glistening crag in sunlit sky,
'Mid snowy clouds piled mountains high,
    Were joys to me;
My path was o'er the prairie wide,
Or here on grander mountain side,
    To choose, all free.

The rose that waved in morning air,
And spread its dewy fragrance there,
    In careless bloom,
Gave to my heart its ruddiest hue,
O'er my glad life its color threw
    And sweet perfume.

Now changed the scene and changed the eyes,
That here once looked on glowing skies,
　　Where summer smiled;
These riven trees, this wind-swept plain,
Now show the winter's dread domain,
　　Its fury wild.

The rocks rise black from storm-packed snow,
All checked the river's pleasant flow,
　　Vanished the bloom;
These dreary wastes of frozen plain
Reflect my bosom's life again,
　　Now lonesome gloom.

The buoyant hopes and busy life
Have ended all in hateful strife,
　　And thwarted aim.
The world's rude contact killed the rose;
No more its radiant color shows
　　False roads to fame.

Backward, amidst the twilight glow,
Some lingering spots yet brightly show
　　On hard roads won,
Where still some grand peaks mark the way
Touched by the light of parting day
　　And memory's sun.

But here thick clouds the mountains hide,
The dim horizon, bleak and wide,
　　No pathway shows,
And rising gusts, and darkening sky,
Tell of the night that cometh nigh,
　　The brief day's close.

From *A Library of American Literature*, edited by Edmund C. Stedman and Ellen M. Hutchinson, vol. 7 (New York: Charles L. Webster and Co., 1890), pp. 189-190.

NOTES ABOUT THE AUTHORS

Adams, James Barton, was a popular newspaper versifier who used western subjects and western dialect and signed himself "Postscript Man" while writing a column for the Denver *Post* in the late nineties and the early nineteen hundreds. He died in Vancouver, Washington, in 1918, at the age of seventy-five. As a volunteer in the Civil War, from his native Ohio, as an Indian fighter from 1873 to 1877 on the plains of Nebraska, Kansas, and Wyoming, and as a volunteer telegrapher in the United States service at the time of his death, he lived a full and useful life.

Anonymous has more listings than any other single author in this collection. The amount of unsigned verse published in early western newspapers and magazines testifies to the modesty of frontier poets. According to modern standards much of this work is poor art; some of it, however, still carries a touch of humor or of old-time flavor and so is worth preserving.

Barker, S. Omar, now living near Sapello, New Mexico, is a prolific author of western stories and poems. Born in 1894 and educated in the public schools of New Mexico and in the New Mexico Normal University (now Highlands University), in Las Vegas, he has worked at ranching, teaching, newspaper writing, publicity, and forestry. After nineteen months overseas in World War I, he was elected to the New Mexico legislature. His verse may be found in *Vientos de las Sierras* (1924) and in *Buckaroo Ballads* (1928), as well as in many magazines and anthologies.

Benton, Frank, was a Wyoming cowboy and cattleman. In 1903, when he published his humorous account of the trials and tribulations of stockmen shipping cattle to market by railroad cattle trains, *Cowboy Life on the Sidetrack,* he wrote that he had been "a cowboy and worked with the cowboys for thirty-two years." Although not a poet, Benton inserted in his book one amusing passage in verse that has been culled for this anthology.

Brininstool, Earl Alonzo, was born in Warsaw, New York, in 1870, but moved to Los Angeles in 1895. After fifteen years of newspaper work he turned to free lance writing. In addition to poems about the cowboy, he has contributed notably to the history of the Old West, including accounts of Indian life and warfare. He collaborated with Dr. Grace Raymond Hebard, of the University of Wyoming, in writing *The Bozeman Trail* (1922).

Butler, William T., a contributor to Harper's *New Monthly Magazine* in 1867, is otherwise unknown to posterity.

Cameron, Don, is a mystery. His undated volume of poetry, *Satire of a Prospector,* carries no place of publication; but a supposed quotation from "The Leadville News Dispatch, 1880" which serves as a preface reads in part as follows: " 'Prospector' is a typical '79 miner. His specialty is satire. He writes whenever the spirit moves him. . . . These are pen pictures upon which the selfish saints and sinners of the world may look and behold their own image." Since a copy of this volume which turned up in a Denver bookstore a few years ago contains an attached pamphlet of poems, entitled *Theology—Wealth and Misery,* by D. B. Cameron (Denver, 1925), it is safe to say that author Cameron belongs to the twentieth century rather than to the boom days of Leadville, Colorado. Still, he writes about mining customs authentically.

Canterbury, (Pvt.) George, a member of "Company C—Regiment Cavalry" was a part of the escort for James F. Meline when he made "a summer tour through Kansas, Nebraska, Colorado, and New Mexico, in the year 1866." Whether or not he ever again burst into poetry is unknown to the present editor.

Carr, Robert V., contributor of cowboy verse to numerous magazines, forty or fifty years ago, published a volume entitled *Black Hills Ballads,* in Denver, 1902, with an "author's note" from Whitewood, South Dakota. A second volume, *Cowboy Lyrics,* privately published in 1908, was designed for distribution "among his friends in the western cattle country." An augmented edition was republished in 1912 with an "author's note" from Los Angeles.

Chapman, Arthur, was born in Rockford, Illinois, in 1873. After working as a reporter on the Chicago *Daily News* (1895-1898), he came to Denver and served as reporter and columnist on the Denver *Republican* (1898-1913) and as managing editor on the Denver *Times* (1916-1919). Then he went to New York to write for the New York *Herald-Tribune.* While in Denver he composed the famous poem, "Out Where the West Begins," to answer a common query and to fill up his column. This poem gave the title to one of his two collections of verse, published in 1917; the other one was *Cactus Center* (1921).

226

The Story of Colorado (1925) and *The Pony Express* (1932) are his contributions to popular history. He died in 1935.

Chittenden, William Lawrence ("Larry"), born in Montclair, New Jersey, in 1862, came to Texas in 1887 and bought a ranch near Anson. Known as the "poet-ranchman," his book *Ranch Verses* (1893) was in its sixteenth edition at his death in 1934. He illustrated his volume with photographs of his ranch and of his ranch house.

Coburn, Wallace D., wrote as follows in the preface to his *Rhymes from a Round-Up Camp* (1899): "My characters are taken from real life, as I have myself seen it during many years spent on the range, in town, in camp and elsewhere with the wildest of wild cowpunchers, and it is needless to say that I have always found these the bravest, best-hearted and most generous set of men, taken as a whole, that it has been my good fortune to find myself associated with." His book was illustrated by his old friend, Charles M. Russell.

Crawford, John Wallace ("Captain Jack"), cultivated the appearance and the reputation of "the poet scout," using as frontispiece for his volumes of poems his own portrait, showing shoulder-length hair, a Buffalo Bill moustache and beard, and a broad-brimmed western hat. Much of his poetry is quite tame, however, as is his prose sketch, "A Chapter for Boys," which tells how he promised his mother on her dying bed that he would never drink intoxicants and that boys should not read dime novels for such would lead them to a life of crime. In 1908, the Roycrofters of East Aurora published a deluxe edition of Crawford's *The Broncho Book, Being Buck-Jumps in Verse*, also tame.

Crawford, Vesta Pierce (Mrs. Arthur L. Crawford), a native of Salt Lake City, was educated at Brigham Young University, Stanford University, and the University of Wyoming. Besides much magazine verse, she has written many articles and some short stories. She resides in Salt Lake City.

Crouch, Pearl Riggs, was born in Bowen, Illinois, studied for two years at California Normal School in San Diego, engaged in newspaper work in California, spent a decade on a Colorado plains homestead, helped to edit a community weekly newspaper, and wrote articles, stories, and verse for many periodicals. After her marriage, she resided at Fort Collins, Colorado, and then at Ashland, Oregon.

Detrick, Daisy L. (Mrs. Herbert Detrick), has spent all except the first year of her life in Colorado. Since she did not piece quilts nor do tatting, she decided to write verses for relaxation. A past-president of the Poetry Society of Colorado, she still writes poetry as a hobby. Rearing and educating her five boys and taking care of her home in Denver have been her serious occupations.

Dillenback, John D., was editor of the Denver *Times* seventy years ago. In 1892-93 he was editor and proprietor of a weekly illustrated journal, *The Coloradan.* In his spare time he wrote stories and verse.

Drannan, Captain William F., "went to the plains when fifteen years old," with Kit Carson, according to his autobiography, *Thirty-one Years on the Plains and in the Mountains.* His experiences as scout for Crook, Connor, Wheaton, and other United States Army leaders are further treated in his second book, *Captain W. F. Drannan, Chief of Scouts, As Pilot to Emigrant and Government Trains, Across the Plains to the Wild West of Fifty Years Ago* (Chicago, 1910). He described his own heroic feats in glowing terms, resorting to verse only a few times.

Ferril, Thomas Hornsby, was born and reared in Denver, Colorado. A graduate of Colorado College, he gained experience as radio officer in World War I, as writer on various newspapers in Denver, and as public relations and advertising man for the Great Western Sugar Company. A frequent contributor of poetry to quality magazines, he has published three collected editions: *High Passage, Westering,* and *Trial by Time.* His knowledge of the West and his love for it are evident in many of his poems.

Field, Eugene, arrived in Denver in the summer of 1881, at the age of thirty-one. There he served as editor on the old Denver *Daily Tribune,* wrote his "nonpariel" column of verse and humorous prose for two years, published his first book, a pamphlet edition of *The Tribune Printer* (December, 1881), and then left for Chicago and national fame. But he continued to consider himself a Westerner, until his death in 1895. Many of his poems reflect a boisterous, frontier spirit, matching the practical jokes that he loved to play on friends and enemies alike.

Frémont, John Charles, is still famous for his western explorations. Few know that he ever wrote a poem, one that expresses the anticlimax of his later years. Politics and California gold promised much to him, but proved fickle. Numerous place names on the map of the United States testify to his lasting influence.

Fynn, Arthur J., at one time superintendent of the Denver Public Schools, wrote the Colorado state song, "Where the Columbines Grow," officially adopted in 1915. He also developed many theories about the Indian, in his book *The American Indian as Product of Environment* (1907).

Gibbons, J. J., was a pioneer missionary priest to the mining regions of the San Juan country, in southwestern Colorado, in the nineties. There he picked up some good burro tales and developed such an appreciation of this faithful little companion to prospectors that he composed the elaborate poetic tribute included in this anthology.

Goldrick, O. J., eccentric but admired pioneer school teacher in the Pikes Peak region, arrived in Denver in the summer of 1859, having worked his way across the plains as a bull-whacker. It is reported that, in place of profanity, he urged along the oxen with Latin phrases learned at Trinity College, Dublin. Known as "the Professor," he was in demand as occasional poet, orator, local historian, and arbiter of men's fashions. Abandoning teaching for journalism, after a short time, he edited the weekly *Rocky Mountain Herald* until his death on November 25, 1882.

Gower, Jean Milne, came to Colorado with her parents in 1871, from Iona, Michigan. In 1890 she became the wife of John H. Gower, organist and choirmaster of Denver's Episcopal cathedral. Until Mr. Gower's death in 1922, they were active in artistic circles, helping to establish the Poetry Society of Colorado. Mrs. Gower conducted a column of prose and verse in the *Rocky Mountain News,* "The Kaleidoscope," including much about the Old West and its Indians.

Greenleaf, Lawrence N., was a prominent early poet and Masonic leader in Denver. Although he wrote primarily for a local audience, he did have a collection of poetry published in New York, in 1868, *King Sham and Other Atrocities in Verse.* This included among other "atrocities," "Pike's Peakers of '59," a fairly good satire.

Hafen, Ann Woodbury (Mrs. LeRoy R. Hafen), a native of Utah, is wife of the State Historian of Colorado and a writer in prose and poetry about western subjects. She is a former president of the

Poetry Society of Colorado and of the local chapter of the League of American Pen Women.

Hanson, Joseph Mills, was a prolific writer on western subjects a generation ago. Born in Yankton, South Dakota, in 1876, he saw service in the South Dakota National Guard in 1916-17 and in the United States Army in 1917-19, ending as Captain and Adjutant in charge of the Historical Section of the General Staff. In addition to *Frontier Ballads* he wrote *With Sully Into the Bad Lands, the Historical Pageant of Yankton* (1916), and *The Conquest of the Missouri, Being the Story of the Exploits of Captain Grant Marsh* (1909; reprinted 1946).

Hay, John Mitton, the secretary and biographer of Lincoln, is known to poetry readers for his *Pike County Ballads,* 1871. His tribute to Miles Keogh's horse should appeal to all horse lovers and students of western history.

Hersey, Harold, according to the jacket blurb of *Singing Rawhide* (1926), is "an American Robert W. Service. He writes of breezy cowboys and western ranges, of gun-play and heart-play. His rhymes are strong, his rough humor irresistible." He was to magazine verse what Bill Hart was to the movies.

Hills, Elijah Clarence, a professor at Colorado College, Colorado Springs, included his own tribute "To Pike's Peak" in his college's publication, *The Pike's Peak Region in Song and Myth,* explaining that "the lyrics and myths in this little volume were read before the Phi Beta Kappa Society of Colorado College during commencement week of 1912."

Holme, Jamie Sexton (Mrs. Peter Hagner Holme), moved to Denver upon her marriage in 1914, from her native Hazelhurst, Mississippi. A contributor of lyrics to many poetry magazines, she included in them vivid, emotional responses to western scenery as well as to more universal subjects.

Howard, Sarah Elizabeth, came to Greeley, Colorado, in 1877. There she served for many years as a cultural leader. Her *Pen Pictures of the Plains* (1902), was illustrated by photographs of scenes along the Cache La Poudre River, of members of the Nathan C. Meeker family, of noteworthy buildings in Greeley, and of mountain landscapes. Her photograph appeared in *Representative Women of Colorado,* Denver, 1914.

Jackson, Helen Hunt, was born in Amherst, Massachusetts, in 1831. Coming to Colorado Springs for her health in 1873, she met and married William S. Jackson of that city, in 1875, thenceforth considering Colorado her home, until her death in 1885. Already a famous author, she drew subjects for prose sketches, fiction, and poetry from her new surroundings. Visits to California gave her materials for *A Century of Dishonor* (1881) and *Ramona* (1884). Her grave on Cheyenne Mountain became such a tourist lure that her family eventually removed her remains to a quiet cemetery in Colorado Springs.

Judy, Scott, was just an old-time prospector who tried with his partner, "Doc" Hammond, to put their experiences into verse.

King, Alfred Castner, turned to writing poetry as an escape from the limited world of the blind. In the preface to *Mountain Idylls and Other Poems* (Chicago, 1901) he wrote from Ouray, Colorado: "On the 17th of March, A.D,. 1900, occurred an accident in the form of a premature mining explosion which banished the light of the Colorado sun from his eyes forever, adding the almost insurmountable barrier of total and hopeless blindness to those of limited means and insufficient education." He dedicated another of his collections, *The Passing of the Storm and Other Poems* (1907), "To a rapidly disappearing class, the pioneer prospectors." This volume is illustrated by photographs of scenes in the San Juan region.

Knibbs, Henry Herbert, was born of American parents in Niagara Falls, Ontario, Canada, in 1874. After Ridley College, Ontario, and Harvard, he traveled and lived in Arizona, New Mexico, and California, writing many western stories and poems. Among his books of verse are *Songs of the Trail* (1920), *Saddle Songs* (1922), and *Songs of the Last Frontier* (1930). He died in 1945.

Kuykendall, John M., crossed the plains in a wagon in 1866 with his mother, wife of Judge W. L. Kuykendall, who had already come ahead to Denver. He edited his father's reminiscenes, *Frontier Days,* 1917, which tells of life on a Wyoming ranch and of cattle business in Denver. Judge Kuykendall was one of the pioneer promoters of western horse shows and rodeos.

Leahy, Jack, was one of the old die-hards to be found occasionally in ghost towns that once were prosperous mining camps. The last inhabitant and therefore "mayor" of Ashecroft, Jack composed and recited poems reflecting the "good old days." Unfortunately few of his verses have survived.

Lindberg, Gene, was born and reared in Pueblo, Colorado, coming to Denver to become a journalist in 1921. Transferring from the old Denver *Times* to the Denver *Post* in 1929, he collaborated for twenty years with the artist Paul Gregg in turning out a weekly combination of vivid paintings of western scenes and human interest verse commenting on these scenes. Gene not only continues to write verse for the *Post,* but he turns his hand to many other journalistic tasks, such as explaining new developments in science.

McGrew, A. O., sometimes called "the wheelbarrow man," set out for the Pikes Peak gold region in the autumn of 1858, pushing before him a wheelbarrow containing his blankets and other provisions for the long trip across the plains. Fortunately, the Larimer party from Kansas overtook him and brought him on into the Cherry Creek diggings. Having agreed to write letters to the newspapers back home, he sent to an Omaha newspaper an eloquent account of Denver's first Christmas celebration, including the poem which he wrote for the occasion.

Mayer, Frank H., in his autobiographical paper "Coals from My Campfire," given before the Denver Posse of the Westerners in 1946, told many interesting stories concerning his ninety-six years of wandrings and adventures. He came to the West, from his native Louisiana, as a young man eager to hunt buffalo. After traveling in many lands he came back to Colorado to spend his last years alone, in a cabin near Fairplay.

Miller, Nellie Burget (Mrs. Lucas A. Miller), was born in Fayette, Iowa, in 1875, soon after her mother arrived there in a covered wagon. In 1894 she married a college classmate who became a physician; in 1908 she moved with him to Colorado Springs, where she has since resided. In 1923 she was appointed Poet Laureate of Colorado by the governor. In *Earthen Bowls* (1924) and *The Sun Drops Red* (1947) she treats many different subjects. In a recent letter she wrote, "If I have contributed anything distinctive to the great composite picture of Colorado it will be found in these pictures of the dry-farming eastern plains as I saw them forty years ago."

Monroe, Arthur W., now a resident of Sunset Beach, California, is the son of a former Colorado newspaper man. From his book, *San Juan Silver,* 1940, we learn the following: "As a United States Ranger, Mesa Verde National Park, from 1923 to 1926, he learned of the Cliff Dwellers. . . . As the editor of a special edition of *The Montrose Messenger,* published on September 20, 1922, he gathered a large amount of the data used in this volume. As special writer and interviewer for the Colorado Historical Society during the winter of 1933-34, he gathered the biographies of one hundred and fifty pioneers of the Western Slope." A pamphlet volume of his verse, *Sunshine and Shadow,* was published in Montrose, about 1945.

Neihardt, John G., born in Illinois in 1881 and for many years a resident of Nebraska and of St. Louis, took as his major subject for a writing career, the struggle between the whites and the Indians for possession of the buffalo plains of the West. His *Epic Cycle of the West* contains five book-length narrative poems, covering the history of the trans-Missouri country from 1822 to 1890: *The Song of Hugh Glass* (1915), *The Song of Three Friends* (1919), *The Song of the Indian Wars* (1925), *The Song of the Messiah* (1936), and *The Song of Jed Smith* (1941). Perhaps his is the most ambitious attempt yet made to put western history into poetic form.

Pike, Albert, came west along the Santa Fe Trail in 1831, stopping in Santa Fe as a store clerk for a year before joining a band of trappers working out of Taos. Going to Arkansas a little later he became a school teacher and then editor of the *Arkansas Advocate,* of Little Rock. Most of his later years he practiced law in Arkansas and in Washington, D. C., but he continued writing both poetry and prose throughout his lifetime.

Prather, Private W. H., was moved to poetry at least once by his experience in the Indian wars, at the time of the Ghost Dance craze. He was a Negro member of Troop "I" of the 9th Cavalry Regiment.

Richardson, Marion Muir (Mrs. M. M. Richardson Ryan), was brought by her parents from Chicago to Gilpin County, Colorado, soon after her birth, in 1859. At the Indian outbreak in 1864, the family went East but returned three years later and settled in 1870 at Morrison. She contributed to and worked on several Denver publications, publishing in eastern journals frequently, also. After her marriage in 1886, she moved with Mr. Ryan to southern Utah.

Rigby, Ralph, is known now only as the contributor of a stray poem to an old Cheyenne newspaper.

Robertson, Clyde (Mrs. William E. Robertson), has won many prizes and honors for her poems and other literary contributions. Born in Indiana, she lived for a time in Oklahoma and Missouri. Since 1909 Colorado has been her home. Among her books are *They Rise Accusing* (1930), *Fool's Gold* (1934), and *Fifty Famous Women* (1936). Her varied experiences include touring as an opera singer and residing in the Leadville mining region.

Sage, Rufus, was a romantic visitor to the Rocky Mountain West in the fur trade period. As a result of his tours in 1841-44 he wrote *Rocky Mountain Life* (1846), containing a number of poems inspired by the scenery and the free life of the frontier. He spent the winter of 1842-43 on the South Platte River below Cherry Creek, near what is now Denver.

Sherwood, Rupe, was buried at Fairplay, Colorado, on August 30, 1931. At his request his grave was next to the monument erected as a tribute to his faithful friend of many years, "Prunes—a Burro, 1867-1930."

Shipp, Judge E. Richard, came to Casper, Wyoming, as a young lawyer from Illinois, in 1905, at a time when cattlemen-sheepmen feuds were blazing. As prosecuting attorney of Natrona County he had many cases dealing with livestock. His spare-time, privately printed verses won him the unofficial title "Poet Laureate of Wyoming." *Intermountain Folk: Songs of Their Days and Ways* appeared in 1922, and *Rangeland Melodies,* in 1923.

Simpson, George S., moved West from St. Louis in 1835-36, to become a prominent trader and merchant in Colorado and New Mexico. He married a Mexican girl in Taos, New Mexico, in 1842. Later he served with Captain Marcy, together with Jim Baker, on the expedition which relieved General Johnston's army in the Utah campaign of 1857. His final home site was near Trinidad, Colorado.

Small, Floyd B., assured the reader of his *Autobiography of a Pioneer,* Seattle, 1916, that it is "an account of the personal experiences of the author from 1867 to 1916. . . it is all truth." This series of prose sketches includes "My First Buffalo Chase" and other adventure stories, as well as the bull-whacker song quoted in this anthology.

Spencer, Mrs. Lilian White, moved from Albany, New York, to Denver with her parents when she was quite young. At sixteen she was writing for the Denver *Post,* of which her father was dramatic critic. Her poetry and plays won many prizes and wide recognition. Her *Pageant of Colorado* was presented before large crowds in the Denver Municipal Auditorium in 1927; and her Pueblo Indian opera, the *Sun Bride,* was given in the outdoor Red Rocks theater, near Denver, in 1935. *Arrowheads* (1929), a collection of verse, illustrates her interest in Indian culture and in western themes.

Sproull, Lyman H., voluminous poet of Cripple Creek, Colorado, in the nineties, wrote as follows in the Preface to *Camp and Cottage: Poems* (Franklin, Ohio, 1896) : "There are many kind, true and appreciative hearts in the camps and cottages of the Rockies, whose friendly faces brighten the rugged desolation of the mountain trail, the monotony of the secluded ranch, and the gloominess of the chambered mine. It is among them that the author lives and labors; it is in the daily lives of them that he sees the joys and sorrows which he strives to portray; and it is to them that he respectfully dedicates his book." Additional books of poetry by Sproull are *Hours at Home* (St. Louis, 1895), *Snowy Summits* (St. Louis, 1898), *In the Land of the Columbine* (Chicago, 1900), and *Mt. of the Holy Cross* (Pueblo, 1947).

"Sunset Joe" preferred to remain unknown to fame. His real name does not appear in his little pamphlet of verse, printed by the Ouray, Colorado, *Herald.*

Taylor, John W., author of "Chipeta's Ride," may be the man of that name whose obituary appeared in the Denver *Post,* November, 1915. If so, he was born in Ireland in 1851, came to the United States in 1870, and owned the Mary Murphy mine at St. Elmo, Colorado, for many years, moving to Denver when the mine was sold to an English company in 1909. More likely, he was someone else, now unidentifiable except as a contributor of newspaper verse.

Vaughn, Frank E., was for many years manager of the Leadville, Colorado, Publishing and Printing Company, which owned and conducted two newspapers in the once-booming mining town. In his preface to *The Spirit of Leadville in Verse* (1929), Mr. Vaughn wrote: "Covering a period of nearly fifty years the writer has inflicted on the people of Leadville through the medium of various newspapers (mostly the Herald Democrat) spasms of rhyme that at times met with the approval of a limited number of his fellow citizens." He spent his last years in retirement in Denver.

Vestal, Stanley (Walter Stanley Campbell), was born in Kansas in 1887. After graduation from Southwestern State Normal School in Oklahoma in 1908, he went to Oxford University for three years as a Rhodes Scholar. After service in the United States Army, 1917-19, he occupied various educational positions before becoming professor of English at the University of Oklahoma, in charge of the professional writing program. He is the author of numerous books of biography, fiction, and popular history, usually dealing with the West.

Warman, Cy (1855-1914), a native of Illinois, came West in the early eighties to be a locomotive engineer on the Denver and Rio Grande Railroad. Later he turned to newspaper work and railroad publicity, the latter taking him to the East, to Europe, and even to Asia. His song poem "Sweet Marie," about the wife he wooed from his engine cab, and his verses about the roaring mining town of Creede, were at one time exceedingly popular. Selections from his *Frontier Stories* (1898) are reprinted in *Literature of the Rocky Mountain West* (1939), edited by Levette J. Davidson and Prudence Bostwick.

Wason, Mrs. Harriet L., was born in England, educated in Pennsylvania, and married to Major Martin V. Wason, of Wagon Wheel Gap, Colorado. She lived in Colorado for thirty years, before her death on August 16, 1904. Her very literate, verse *Letters from Colorado* (1887) was written in the character of a young Harvard man who had come West for a vacation and had been so entranced with the life and scenery that he remained permanently.

Westcott, Judge Joseph L., was mustered out of the Union cavalry in 1865, suffering from inflammatory rheumatism, for the relief of which he came to Hot Sulphur Springs, Colorado. Cured of his illness, he became the first white settler at Grand Lake, Colorado, in 1867, and the first postmaster there in 1877. Here he lived until 1914, often isolated by severe winters, "keeping batch" in a log cabin, and selling lots along the lake from time to time.

Whitney, J. Ernest, was a Connecticut man, Yale graduate, and instructor in English literature, who because of ill health spent the last four years of his life (1889-93) in Colorado Springs. Two of his volumes of verse concerned his new home, *Pictures and Poems of the Pikes Peak Region* and *Myths and Legends of the Manitou*.

Wood, Stanley, was eminently successful as a newspaperman, a railroad publicist, a playwright, author of comic opera libretti, and writer on western travel. Born in Peru, Ohio, educated at Oberlin College. and a New York journalist before coming to Colorado Springs as city editor of the *Gazette* (1879-82), Wood was chief of the literary bureau of the Denver and Rio Grande Railroad (1882-89), before taking charge of Colorado's outstanding literary weekly *The Great Divide* (1889-94). When that magazine moved to Chicago, he went with it, but economic depression followed it and it ceased publication after a few more years of struggle.

INDEX OF TITLES

INDEX OF AUTHORS

240